Artists' Conceptions of Money

Reinold Widemann

Artists' Conceptions of Money

Money Art and Artificial Money

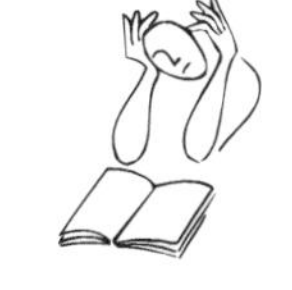

Aspekt Publishers

Cover image (left and backside): Detail from 'Blow'. Archival embossed Inkjet print on 330gsm Somerset Satin paper. 2014
Cover image (right): detail from 'Blast'. Archival embossed Inkjet print on 330gsm Somerset Satin paper. 2017

Artists' Conceptions of Money

Aspekt Publishers | Amersfoortsestraat 27
3769 AD Soesterberg | The Netherlands
info@uitgeverijaspekt.nl | www.uitgeverijaspekt.nl
Coverdesign: Mark Heuveling & Tessa Vermeulen
Lay-out: Paul Timmerman

ISBN: 978-94-6338-428-5
NUR: 640

Content

Intro 9

1 **The mystery of money** 12
Searching for the Soul of the Sign

What is Money?, *Sebastian Siechold*; **THE SOUL OF MONEY,** *Burning money and goods for dead ancestors in China*; **Burning Money and The Joker; Discordianism; Money Burning at the Horse Hospital,** *Jonone100*; **Burning Money,** *the K Foundation*; **Money to burn,** *Dread Scott on Wall Street*; **Hello Bitcoin,** *Geraldine Juárez*; **Provoking Money-Burning Tables: "Too much?",** *Alejandro Monge*; **Eating Money,** *Cesare Pietroiusti and Franz Gratwohl.*

2 **The Golden Delusion** 43
Aurum and aura

The Money Changer and His Wife, *Quentin Massijs*; **Tower of Power,** *Chris Burden*; **Easy, Breezy, Beautiful,** *Sylvie Fleury*; **Folkestone Digs,** *Michael Sailstorfer*; **Danaë**

project, *Vadim Zakharov*; **Danaë paintings,** *Gustav Klimt, Titian, Correggio, Rembrandt*; **Annunciation,** *Simone Martini*; **Von Explosionen zu Ikonen,** *Alicja Kwade*; **Soil-erg,** *Claire Pentecost*; **The Cross of Gold,** *Victor Dubreuil*; **Art for Money – Money for Art,** *Leroy Brothers*; **Bright Future Horizons,** *Anna Ihle.*

3 **Evergreen?** 66
Songs of love and hate

Dollar Bills and Dollar Signs, *Andy Warhol*; **Green Dollar Sign on Malevich's Suprematism,** *Alexander Brener*; **One Billion Dollar (Most Expensive Artwork Ever),** *Michael Marcovici*; **100,000 Dollar Wall,** *Hans-Peter Feldmann*; **Money Shark and a whitewashed mural with Dollar Coffins,** *Blu*; **Dollar Skulls,** *Scott Campbell*; **Weapons and Dollars,** *Justine Smith*; **MONEY COLLAGES: Currency Collages,** *Mark Wagner*; **Currency Collages,** *C.K. Wilde*; **MONEYGAMI: Moneygami with dollars: The Plaque,** *Sipho Mabona*; **Moneygami: world leaders in funny hats,** *Yosuke Hasegawa*; **Money-gami: dollar animals, vehicles and mythical creatures,** *Won Park*; **Moneygami with a twist,** *Dan Tague*; **A pyramid of shredded dollars: Evergreen,** *Jason Hughes*; **Moneyball: Power Spheres,** *Alberto Echegaray alias Cayman.*

4 **Art = Money** 98
Art as a currency

TROMPE L'OEIL MONEY: Barrels full of painted bank notes, *Victor Dubreuil*; **Is it real?** *John Haberle, William Michael Harnett, Charles Alfred Meurer*; **Up and down,** *Otis Kaye*; **Pursued by the law,** *J.S.G. Boggs.*

5 **Global exchange** 114
Around the world with currency

Sail Away and Dress Sculptures, *Susan Stockwell*; **Money/Change/Money,** *Timm Ulrichs*; **Artmoney/Change/Money,** *Maria Frisahn*; **The world's garbage,** *Máximo Gonzáles*; **Money for Art,** *Lee Mingwei*; **Cultural Symbols,** *Barton Lidicé Beneš*; **Give me my fucking money!** *William Powhida*; **The artist as a currency converter,** *Dadara*; **Money Maps,** *Justine Smith.*

6 **In Art We Trust** 132
A ring of believers

Dollar bill acceptor, collected money, *Caleb Larson*; **Prada juxtaposed with 99 cent,** *Andreas Gursky*; **Liquid Assets,** *Ori Gersht*; **$49,983 paid and pulped for an Art Degree,** *Thomas Gokey*; **Bankrupt Banks,** *Superflex*; **How to Build Cathedrals, Insertions to Ideological Circuits,**

a golden Thread and a Money Tree, and reducing the value of money to nothing, *Cildo Meireles.*

7 **Time is money** 148
The real price of everything

Time is Money, *Ferdinand Danton, Jr*; **Time/Bank,** *Julieta Aranda and Anton Vidokle*; **Money Watching,** *Cesare Pietroiusti*; **Attention: the new currency,** *Christa Sommerer & Laurent Mignonneau.*

8 **Empire of the imagination** 157
The fiduciary world of money and art

A signed urinal and broken shovels, *Marcel Duchamp, Hans Haacke*; **An immaterial pictorial zone,** *Yves Klein*; **Greed Devours,** *Ralf Kopp*; **Paying people to do crazy things,** *Santiago Sierra*; **Take what you need,** *Lee Lozano, Elana Mann.*

Outro 171

Further reading 173
Endnotes 175

Intro

In 1919 Marcel Duchamp paid his dentist Daniel Tzanck with a check of $ 115, designed by himself. The check was covered by the imaginary *'Teeth's Loan and Trust Company, Consolidated'*, established at Wall Street. The dentist accepted this **Tzanck Check** and by doing so he showed that he considered art as a kind of currency.

Is art a form of money? *Joseph Beuys* wrote **Kunst = Kapital** (Art = Capital) on blackboards and banknotes. And *Damien Hirst* once said that art is the most important currency in the world. Some artists made their own money and paid with it. *JSG Boggs* for instance drew banknotes with a fine pen, put his portrait on them and put them into circulation. With this artificial money he succeeded in buying goods for over a million Euros.

In the past some old masters and modern ones used to make money the subject of their works of art. Beside using money as a source of inspiration, they expressed their views on the meaning of money in their artworks as well. Nowadays a growing number of contemporary artists are producing art in which they critically comment on the meaning of money in our present financialized society. Their artistic comments are useful eye-openers to reconsider the meaning and role of money in modern society.

Money has been the main subject of my interest in my professional career as a lecturer in economics. I wrote some books about banking, international economics and factors influencing interest rates. During my retirement this interest broadened to the more philosophical field of money as a symbol of value. In my recent book *Money is a mind thing, on symbols of value* I added a last chapter on money art and artificial money, as I had come across a number of very inspiring artworks on money on my many visits to exhibitions and manifestations of contemporary art. It led to my search for more money art, a series of lectures on the subject and the request of my publisher Perry Pierik (ASPEKT) to write a book about money art.

The book highlights a selection of the work of about eighty money-artists, but during my investigation I discovered there are many more. I apologize to those artists with often beautiful works of money-art who are not represented in this book, but I had to make a choice to keep it manageable.

It has been a pleasure to work on this book, not the least because of the pleasant e-mail contact with some artists from all over the world, who willingly gave me information and their consent to use some pictures of their art.

My special thanks go to Justine Smith, Mark Wagner, Geraldine Juárez, Yosuke Hasegawa, Jason Hughes, Jonathan Harris and Thomas Gokey.

1

The mystery of money

Searching for the Soul of the Sign

What is money? *Sebastian Siechold*

"To whom it may concern,
For a considerable time now, I am concerned with a question I hereby seek to have answered.
What is money?

Sincerely,

Sebastian Siechold."

This letter was written by the German artist *Sebastian Siechold* (b. 1982) to 46 European National Banks in the corresponding national language.[1] It was an ongoing project during 2012-2014. He received 21 replies. What did he do with them? He didn't open the envelopes, but showed them unopened in some exhibitions. Before, in 2012 he had written the same kind of letters to the 11 largest Swiss Banks and had also exhibited their unopened written replies. Wasn't he curious to learn what money really is? Well, he might know the answer himself, but that was not the point of this artistic action. In relation to the way we use money, he says: *Perhaps everybody knows that money is only a representation of agreements between people, but we behave like the sign would be what it signifies. In my work I try to bring out the magical dimension of money itself, the way we use it and how it functions in different systems. (...) It's not my effort to explain, what money is, but to create situations, which give people a possibility to think about the complexity of money.*[2]

The art of Sebastian Siechold represents a systematic exploration of money in all its contexts and symbolic aspects. In this scope he also collected a number of money jokes which he put on handmade money paper, inscribed with typewriter and displayed behind acrylic glass (14,8 x 21 cm). Here I quote two of these jokes:

1. *Mc Donald comes home from work furious and out of breath.*
His wife asks him, why he is so furious.
He responds: "I have barely missed the bus and then I ran closely all the way behind the bus."
"Be happy" responds his wife, "so you saved 50 pence passage money!"
"Yes you are right, but if I would have been running behind a taxi, I would have saved 5 pounds!"

2. *A man enters a bank in Zurich and says he wants to make a journey and needs a credit on 5000 CHF. As deposit he wants to give his Rolls Royce.*

The bank agrees and parks the car in the secure basement garage. Two weeks later the man comes back and repays the 5000 CHF plus 12 CHF interest.

The bank assistant takes the money and comments: "We noticed that you are a multimillionaire. Why did you need a credit on 5000 CHF?"

The man responds: "Where else could I have parked my car near the Bahnhofstrasse for two weeks for only 12 CHF?"

If you like to read more of his money jokes, visit the website.[3]

Another kind of conceptual artistic money joke of Siechold was *The One-Pfennig Exchange* action he did in 2010. Unlike in other European countries, there was no limit in Germany for the exchange of old currency (the German mark) into euro's. The exchange rate was 1.95583 : 1. In order to determine how the relevant authorities would handle the smallest unit of the German mark, Siechold asked the German Federal Bank to exchange his one-pfennig coin into euros. Although it was essentially an impossible exchange, in response to his request he received a check in the value of one cent, thus receiving the best possible exchange rate of 1 : 1.

THE SOUL OF MONEY, *Burning money and goods for dead ancestors in China*

Another one of the money artworks of Sebastian Siechold is the money machine he made to burn money for dead ancestors in China. In China, people are convinced that the dead continue their lives after death and will be in use of money over there. At first they arrive in a kind of Hell, where the *Lord of the Earthly Court*, **Yan Wang**, judges them. This Lord, once a living Chinese Emperor, is also known as the *Emperor of the Afterworld* or the *Lord of Hell.* After this judgment, they are either escorted to heaven or sent into the maze of underworld levels and chambers to atone for their sins.[4] People believe that even in this earthly court, spirits need money. For this purpose, people in China make ghost or spirit money. Because the Lord of Hell is reigning over the Afterworld, the banknotes used for burning are also called *Hell Banknotes*. This isn't real money, but artificial money. It's a Taoist ritual, in which this artificial money is sent to deceased relatives in the hereafter, by being burnt. They need this money for their daily needs. And the life beyond the grave isn't cheap. That's why ghost money is supplied in high denominations of 10,000 up to 1 billion Yuan, but also in dollars or other currencies. Common on the faces of all Hell Banknotes is the image of the Emperor of the Afterworld.

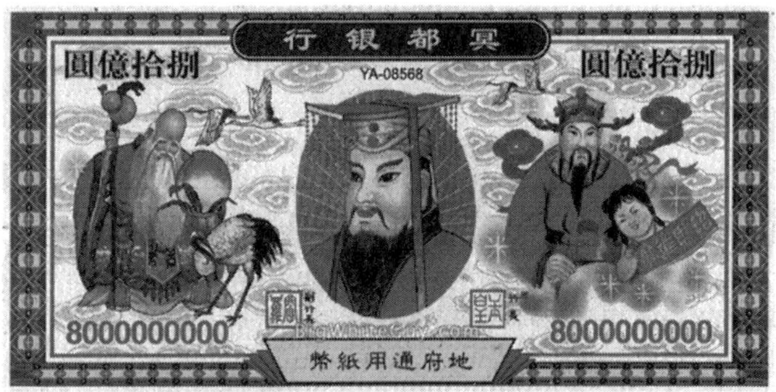

Hell Bank Note, China, with the image of the Emperor of the Afterworld.

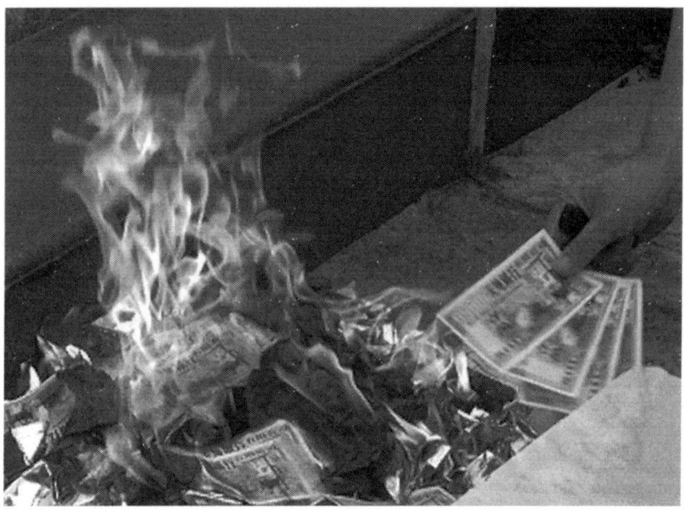

Hell Bank Note burning.

Because electronic payment to the hereafter doesn't exist, burning money is the quickest alternative to pay deceased loved ones – although nowadays checks and paper credit cards are used as well.

But what the Chinese send to their ancestors is not restricted to ghost money. On specific occasions, they also take paper replicas of luxury goods, gold, and everyday items and burn them to serve their ancestors. In 2010 Sebastian Siechold met Mrs. Chen Da Jie, an old lady whose family had mastered the art of making such paper replicas for generations. She created an ATM (automated teller machine) for him for 400 yuan. The artist then burned it in order to serve its purpose.

The *DOX Centre for Contemporary Art* in Prague made a beautiful exhibition on this ***Soul of Money***,[5] and in the *Staatliche Kunstsammlungen Dresden* was a similar show in 2015, called the ***Supermarket of the Dead***, made up by *Wolfgang Schleppe*.[6] The paper replicas of money and goods that are ritually burned *have recently undergone a kind of transformation,* Schleppe says, *in which imitations of traditional objects have been superseded by replicas of consumer goods found in western shopping habits. (...) all today's globalised brand consumption fetishes, Gucci bags, Prada shoes, mobile phones, Apple computers and even Heineken beer cans and life-size cars, is committed to the flames as a tribute to the ancestors.*

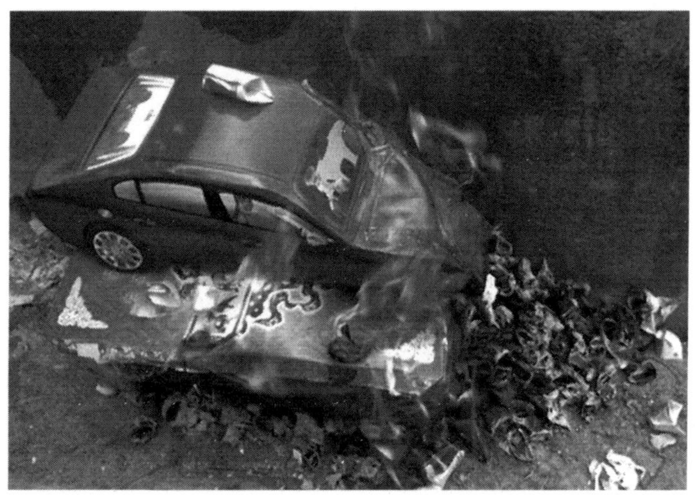

Burning a paper car for the dead in China.

The Supermarket of the Dead displayed *a mountain of these strangely familiar yet somehow alien goods. (...) The West's worship of brand names and designer labels can be discerned and linked to a cult which is almost two thousand years old. One becomes aware too of the quasi-religious fetishism inherent in the consumption of branded product, (...) – and hence a theurgic relationship.*

So, when Sebastian Siechold burned a paper ATM for his ancestors, he used an old Chinese spiritual tradition to make an artistic statement about the transcendent soul of money.

Searching for the soul of the money sign, we must look beyond the material signifiers of exchange value. Those material signifiers are coins and banknotes. What can money artists do to free or separate the sign from the signifier? Well, they tried to do so in several ways: by eating, burning, cutting, folding, knitting, gluing, drawing, sculpturing, crucifying, redecorating or revaluing the money signifiers for instance or by making money collages, stamping, hammering and inserting inscriptions, making origami artworks with banknotes and even treating money with acid. You will learn more about these applications in this book. I start with some artists who are in the business of money-burning.

Burning money and The Joker

Why should anyone want to burn money? In 2013 *John Higgs* mentioned ten reasons.[7] Here's his top 10:

1. To Frighten
2. Ostentation
3. Protest
4. Spite
5. Currency validation
6. Cracking up
7. Becoming Sane
8. War
9. Forgiveness
10. Housekeeping

Is money burning by (money) artists fitting in one or more of these motives? Let's try to find out.

A famous example of the first motive was the fire action of **The Joker** in the Batman movie *The Dark Knight* from 2008. Can this film scene be considered as an example of money art? I think so, because movie is an artistic medium and in this scene an artistic message on burning money is sent. That's what The Joker himself says after he sets fire in a considerable stack of cash: his crime spree is *not about money... it's about sending a message*. What message? Higgs says that *It is, clearly, that people should be afraid of him.* And David Mullich writes: *The Joker, as depicted in Christopher Nolan's film is an anarchist (...) His goal is to bring about chaos in the world. By burning the money, he is demonstrating that he does not care about money; he just wants to see the world burn. By demonstrating that he cannot be bought – that is he cannot be controlled – The Joker hopes that people lose faith in the rules that bring about order to society, which in turn will accelerate the chaos he hopes to bring to Gotham.*[8]

So, The Joker's purpose is chaos, which means he is a **Discordianist**. What is a Discordianist? As you probably can guess: a follower of the principles of **Discordianism**.

Discordianism

Discordianism is a kind of religion that preaches chaos. This Discordianism is a paradigm based on the book *Principia Discordia*, written by *Greg Hill* with *Kerry Wendell Thornley* in 1963.[9] For this book the two of them were working under the curious pseudonyms *Malaclypse the Younger* and *Omar Khayyam Ravenhurst*. According to *Adam Gorightly*, its primary historian, Discordianism was founded as a parody religion and many people still regard it as such, but some of its adherers utilize it as a legitimate religion, or a metaphor for a governing philosophy. The reasoning goes that, as chaos is the fundamental principle of reality, the supreme being most worthy of worship is *Eris* or *Discordia*, the Goddess of chaos. In the book the worship of *Eris* is encouraged. The Principia Discordia holds three principles: the *Aneristic Principle* (order), the *Eristic Principle* (disorder) and the *notion that both are mere illusions*. It is only by rejecting these principles that you can truly perceive reality. It is difficult to estimate the number of Discordians because they are not required to hold Discordianism as their only belief, and because there is an encouragement to form schisms and cabals.[10]

Are there, besides The Joker, any other Discordians to be found among money burning artists? In other words, is it their intention to shock people with this kind of art and send a message of chaos? Or do they have other motives?

Money Burning at the Horse Hospital, *jonone100*

When people witness money burning, it is always accompanied by some inconvenience or even anxiety and fear for the stability of society. The blogger *jonone100* (Jonathan Harris, 1974) always experienced this discomfort in the audience on seeing him burning money. The artist sometimes refers to himself as the ***Money Burning Guy*** or ***Cosmic Money Engineer***. But is he also a Discordianist? What is his goal when he is burning money?

On Wednesday 23rd October 2013 he burned the twenty pounds sterling note OA37 598019 in public at a *Fortean Society* event in London.[11] The event took place at the Horse Hospital in Bloomsbury, London.

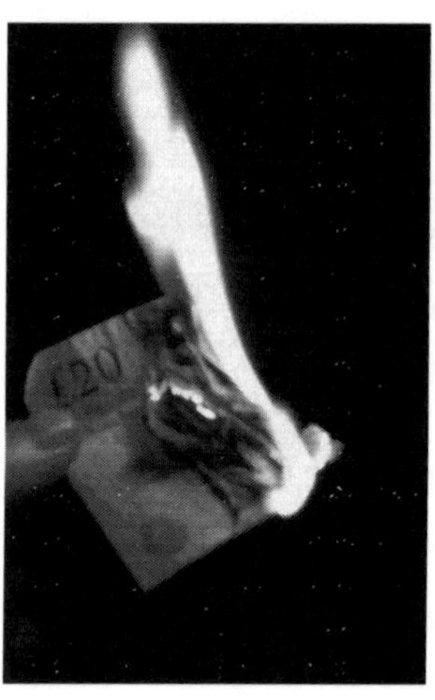

jonone100 burning the twenty pounds sterling note OA37598019 Wednesday 23rd October 2013. (Image courtesy of the artist)

He *sensed a nervousness in the audience* when he set fire to the £20 note, because burning money is taboo. *I didn't really want to interact with the audience during the burning itself,* he said, *so I just kind of zoned out of the comments* he received during the performance. *The only comment that broke to me was* ***How many children in Syria would that save?***, jonone said. That question was repeated during the burning and this repetition bugged him a bit, because it broke his *connection with the ritual.*

Did jonone burn the money to frighten people like The Joker did? No, jonone's money burning was not to frighten people, but to make a statement about the ritual of burning money. So his performance can't be placed in the first category of Higgs. Perhaps in the second: ostentation? After all, he wanted to demonstrate something about the ritual character of burning money. But which ritual did he mean? On a later occasion, in 2016, when he burned money at a festival in Greno Woods, Sheffield, UK, he gave a talk before the ritual and explained the ritual background of money burning in depth in another blog: **Why Burn Money?**[12] In this blog he gives *three key points that I think might help make sense of money burning.* Because I believe he goes to the heart of the matter in this statement, I will quote him extensively:

1. As the ***general equivalent value form*** *money is an ideal sacrament. In other words, the idea that money can be any-*

thing and everything and everything makes burning it – turning it into nothing – especially potent metaphysically, symbolically and magically. By burning money you are, in a sense, burning everything – including yourself (although hopefully, not literally).

2. Related to ***1.****, is the idea that* ***currency was born of ritual sacrifice.*** *Two theories about it are that money evolved from votive offerings or from spits used to distribute the meat of sacrificed animals. Ritual sacrifice was the focal point for a group's social, psychological, and sexual relations, and so economic ideas that conceive of money as a 'social relation' (as opposed to it being 'a thing' or representation of 'a thing') build directly upon these sacrificial foundations. What I try to get across within the ritual itself, is that by making a sacrament of currency we are returning money to its source.*

3. The final and possibly the most important point is about ***the ritual as an act of pure forgiving.*** *I hope that all those who participated – whether or not they burned – experienced this as engendered within the ritual. Money burning is equivalent to pure forgiving because it is* 'giving without receiving.' *Pure forgiveness requires that we forgive the unforgivable. And it is this contradiction or* 'impossibility' *that money burning approaches.*

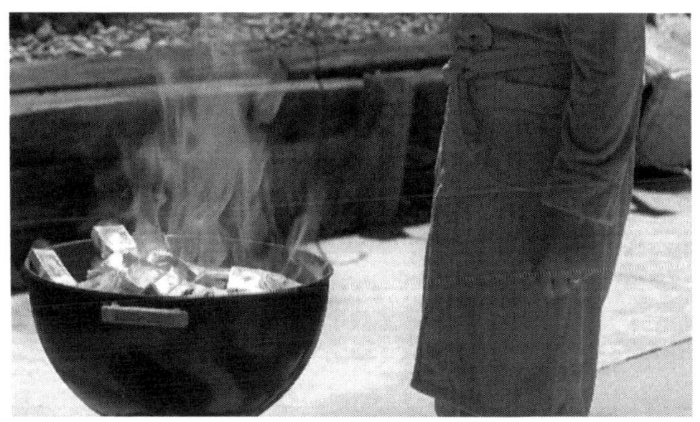

jonone100, burning money. (Image courtesy of the artist)

After reading the third point of jonone's statement, it will be obvious that his motives for burning the money were not at all a matter of ostentation, but to focus our attention to the number nine on the list of Higgs' top ten reasons for money burning: **forgiveness**!

It's about morality, jonone said. *If I had gone up to the bar, bought five beers and tipped the bar man a fiver, I'd have spent £20 but no-one would have mentioned the 'children in Syria'. But I didn't. Because I burned £20 the morality around money came into sharp focus and suddenly my £20 was connected to the suffering of children in Syria.* Because of the disapproving attitude of the public witnessing him burning the money, he got *the plain feeling (...) that I have done something morally wrong.*

So, what might people think when they see someone burning money, I wonder, do they think he is wasting money? Spending it frivolously? No, says Higgs, because according to him wasting money and burning money are two distinct moral categories.

Can jonone100 be considered a Discordian? No, because his aim is not causing chaos like The Joker, but to focus our attention to the morality of money burning. In his blog he speaks of the taboo of money burning, because it's seen as *pure waste, the creation of NOTHING from something.*[13] In his further clarification he pursues this point more deeply and says that *The determination to break a taboo requires a commitment on your behalf.* And: *Money burning is a material change in your relation to money. (...) We experience money through its impact on our mind and bodies. The fear and faith, love and hate, joy and pain we feel around money are its landscape. Money exists within these oppositions. (...) The ones and zeros in banks' computers are a* ***representation*** *of money, not its essence. Its essence is with us, in our experience of being and consciousness. It's not out there in the numbers, it's in here with you and me.*

So, money is a part of ourselves, you could say, and that's why burning money feels like burning a part of ourselves – a kind of sacrifice that hurts.

Burning money, *the K Foundation*

When jonone100 spoke of the morality of burning money, he was also referring to the aforementioned John Higgs, who wrote a book about the **KLF**, a British electronic band of the late 1980's and early 1990's.[14] **The KLF** (Kopyright Liberation Front) was also known as **The Justified Ancients of Mu Mu**, or **The Jams** and **The Timelords.** This band earned so much money, that the two musicians *Bill Drummond* and *Jimmy Cauty* had a problem spending it in a satisfying way. [15] Therefore they decided to burn a million pounds. Why and how?

With the KLF's profit the duo *established the K Foundation and sought to subvert the art world, staging an alternative art award for the worst artist of the year and burning one million pound sterling.* In 1993 they chose a shortlist of four artists, who would be exhibited in The Tate Gallery. This shortlist of named artists was the same as the one for the 1993 Turner Prize, *the controversial annual award given by the UK art establishment to the best young modern artist, which came with a prize of 20,000 pounds.*[16] *Rachel Whiteread* was the winner of the Turner Prize that year, but she was not amused when she was contacted by the K-Foundation and informed that she had won the 40,000 pound prize. She refused to allow her name to be used in the TV advert. So what to do with the money then? Well, the two men of the K Foundation made quite a show of it and started distributing the money amongst a group of 25 witnesses (art critics, journalists, music industry figures, artists etc.). You can read all about it on the website.[17] But this was only the start, because there was a bigger 'problem':

the £1,000,000 they had earned as musicians in The KLF and wanted to get rid of in an artistic way. They decided to nail the money in 50 pound note wads to a large framed board and this became the K-F's first artwork: **'Nailed To The wall'**. All the witnesses were impressed, but one artist complained that it wasn't a work of art, as it wasn't signed. However, the compere Mr. Ball deadpanned this argument with *I think you'll find that every note is signed sir.* The reserve price of the work was set at half the face value of the cash involved. So, **Nailed To The Wall** had a face value of a million, but was for sale at only 500,000 pounds! The catalogue stated: *Over the years the face value will be eroded by inflation, while the artistic value will rise and rise. The precise point at which the artistic value will overtake the face value is unknown. Deconstruct the work now and you double your money. Hang it on a wall and watch the face value erode, the market value fluctuate, and the artistic value soar. The choice is yours.* [18] With this work of art the K Foundation made a simple statement: art is a speculative currency, and vice-versa. *"To put it more bluntly: Art equals Money, and Money equals Art."* (This statement is the subject of chapter 4 in this book: ART = MONEY.)

And what happened to the rest of the money? Did Rachel Whiteread accept her £40,000 from the K Foundation? You can guess the answer. Even worse, Channel 4, who financed the Turner Prize and covered the award ceremony live, made absolutely no mention of the alternative award in the Turner studio discussion and according to the K-F this was *an act of crass cowardice and stupidity by the Channel 4 program makers which confirmed all the points about modern art establishment that the K-F were trying to make.* When, after a last attempt to hand over the prize money to Rachel Whiteread on the steps of the Tate, she refused to accept it, the K-F explained that it would be burnt. But when a K-F operative fumbled with matches and lighter fluid, at the last moment Rachel Whiteread emerged from the Tate and accepted the money, stating *that she would give it as grants to needy artists.* There was a lot of comment and press coverage of the whole event, but after the dust had settled, the K-F still was lumbered up with their artwork **Nailed To The Wall.** For the first six months they tried to get their art exhibition staged. The most likely gallery was the Tate in Liverpool, but unfortunately it didn't come off, so they had to consider other options. *They thought about taking the exhibition across Russia by train, but the cost of insuring a million pounds against robbery by the armed gangs that roam across the Stepps, was too high. They decided that the money was a millstone around their necks, that depressed them. They decided that they would have to really burn the money.*"[19] But how? And where? In public or not? After a full consideration and rambling, they decided to burn the million pounds in an abandoned boathouse on Jura in the middle of the night of the 23rd of August 1994. A K-F operative filmed it, and freelance journalist *Jim Reid* witnessed it. The whole story is told by Reid in an article in The Observer called 'Money to burn'.[20]

You can ask yourself why the K Foundation members Bill Drummond and Jimmy Cauty burned the million quid. Well, it seems they didn't know themselves when they started the action. Drummond said: *It's taken us almost a year to come to terms with what we did. Now we feel we want to try and find out why we did it.* And Cauty added: *We're trying to find out why we did it and we're getting closer all the time. We're trying to get the list down to ten reasons as opposed to 5,000 reasons.*[21] And did they find out at last why they did it? Perhaps: *"We think burning the money was constructive because nobody's ever done it before."* We leave this explanation to your own judgment. And what do you think how the public reacted? Well, *(...) many locals reacted angrily. A lot of people thought it was really wasteful. They thought we should have given it away,* Cauty said, but *that wasn't very interesting to us.*

So far about this striking artistic money burning action of the K Foundation in 1994. You can read much more about it on the aforementioned sites and in the book of John Higgs.

Money to burn, *Dread Scott on Wall Street*

In 2010 the conceptual and performance artist *Dread Scott* (b. 1965) enacted a performance on Wall Street, where he burned dollar bills – singles, fives, tens and twenties, one bill at a time. He started with $250 of his own money and encouraged traders and others on The Street to join him with their own money. Referencing street peddlers of bygone days, he repeatedly sang the words *money to burn*.

As we noticed before, money burning explores a taboo. But according to the artist, his performance *only made physical what happens on stock markets around the globe every day.*[22] His own money of $250 was provided by a grant of the Franklin Furnace Fund.[23] He stated that his performance *alluded to the absurdity of a system based on profit. It's crazy to burn money on the street but it is the height of rationality to have a market where billions of dollars can vanish in an instant and where even houses and food can evaporate. Unlike the 'irrational exuberance' behind closed doors of trading firms, Money to Burn took place in public for all to see. It was the ultimate act of destruction of value – this money was not exchanged for anything.*[24] He added that the unsettling immolation of his performance *highlighted the polarization of wealth and income that exists in the world.* At the performance there was an audience of brokers and tourists present and Scott gave them the option of joining the act. Some recoiled, but others chose to add to the pyre. The performance was planned to last 40 minutes, but police intervened after 25 minutes and stopped the performance 15 minutes later. To which one of the ten reasons to burn money that John Higgs mentioned can the performance of Scott be assigned? Clearly to the number 3 of the list: protest. And I think that number 7 is also applicable here: becoming sane.

Hello Bitcoin, *Geraldine Juárez*

In the previous section we came across artists who occupied themselves with burning paper money, but is it also possible to burn virtual money? Can you burn a bank account? That's a hard thing to do, because digital money is not material money. Bitcoins are a form of digital money stored in a kind of wallet: a Bitcoin wallet. But such a wallet is merely a computer device, an encrypted code, installed on your Smartphone for instance. And when you burn this Smartphone you won't burn this encrypted code, because your private bitcoin key, can be activated on any computer. A private key in the context of bitcoin is a

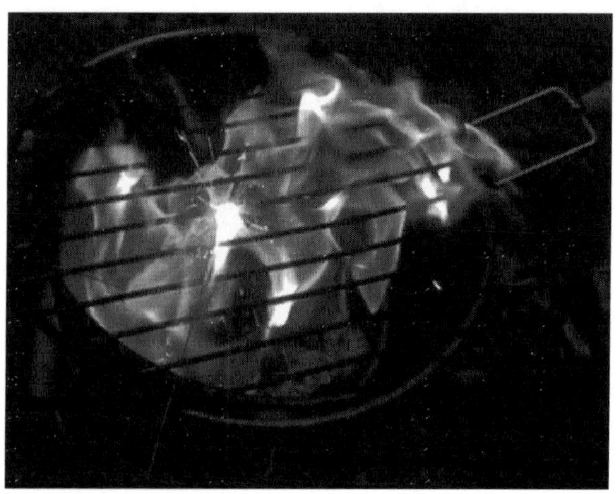

Geraldine Juárez, Hello Bitcoin. (Image courtesy of the artist)

secret number that allows bitcoins to be spent. Every Bitcoin wallet contains one or more private keys, which are saved in the wallet file.

The Mexican born artist *Geraldine Juárez* (1977), living in Sweden, considered this problem and asked herself if bitcoins are real money, when it's not possible to burn them: *"What makes a currency real? When we are able to burn them for real of course."*[25] In her outdoor performance bitcoins were wasted, *post-digital style* she called it. Obviously she explicitly refers to real money as cash. But for the purpose of the digital Bitcoin burning she found a way to do it: she offloaded a Bitcoin wallet with nine milibitcoins (0.00977616 BTC) from her laptop onto a gold painted SD memory card and barbecued it.

But I had my doubts: were these nine milibitcoins really gone after the memory card had been burnt? Because the bitcoins are in the blockchain and if the artist kept a note somewhere of her private bitcoin key, even when she just scrabbled it on a piece of paper, she might be able to recover her bitcoins. So, if you want to destroy your bitcoins forever, you must destroy your private key as wel. Did she do that? I couldn't find any report on this, so I decided to ask her this personally. *I burn all the files in that sd card,* she answered me. *I didn't keep the private key, neither of the second performance I did.*

Problem solved: her bitcoins were definitely gone forever. But you may wonder why she did it. *Jonone100, the K-foundation* and *Dread Scott* all had their reasons, but what was Geraldine Juárez' motivation to burn bitcoins? A blogger using the pseudonym *Granaton* wrote a critical piece on this question.[26] She said that the artist didn't give any explanation for her action. Not a word on the economical crisis for instance or the public rescue of banks, nothing on inflation, the kind of money we are using and no connection to book or witch burning in the old days for instance. Just the burning of bitcoins without any background information. Is that serious? Does a performance like that call for any further comment? I leave the question open.

Does the performance of Geraldine Juárez fit in one of the ten categories mentioned by John Higgs? If so, it might

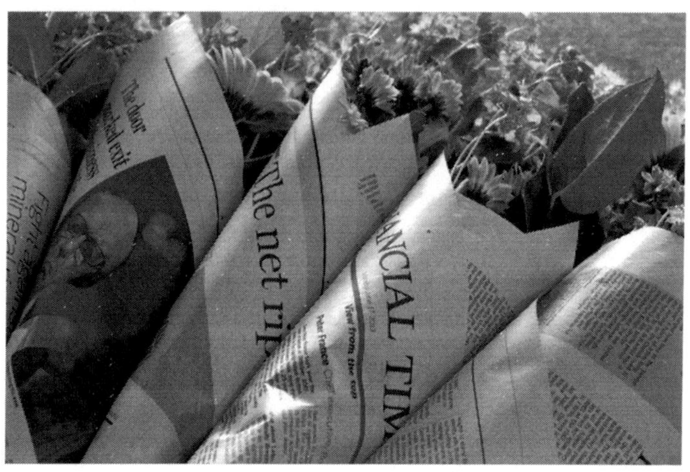

Geraldine Juárez, FT Bouquet (2014). (Image courtesy of the artist)

be number 5: *currency validation*, because the artist pointed out that only real currencies could be burnt and by this burning performance she 'proved' that Bitcoins are real money.

Geraldine Juárez made some other nice money artworks too, like the *FT Bouquet* [27] and *Some People just want to see the Market Crash*.[28]

Provoking Money-Burning Tables: "Too much?",
Alejandro Monge

In my final example of money-burning art I cross the line between Art and Design. The AMARIST atelier[29] presented a series of money-burning tables, called *Too much*. The sculptural tables were made in collaboration with Spanish artist *Alejando Monge* (b. 1988) and *seek to provoke a deep thought about the volatility of money*.[30] The tables are made of glass cubes containing partially burnt 50 euro bills and with a thin bio fuel flame rising above its surface. The artist *meticulously reproduced banknotes from paper using a hyper-realistic technique, and simulated the effect of the burning fire sculpting an petrifying ashes with resin,* it is said on the site.[31] The question that Alejandro Monge is asking is an old one: What is the value of money? And the explanation he gives through his money-burning tables is: *An euro bill by itself is a mere tinted paper representing a figure; 20, 50, 100 ... and has no more value than the time invested to get it. We just seek to exchange it for a desired object or experience. The artwork suggests a reflection about the significance and value of money, time and people. That is the reason why the work is done entirely with paper, hand colored and glued together one by one.* To simulate the effect of the burnt paper without actually using fire, was the most complicated part of the process. If you want to see how it is done, see the video on the aforementioned website.[32]

Now let's have a closer look at two money-eating artists, who tried to approach the soul of the money sign by eating the signifier.

Eating Money, *Cesare Pietroiusti and Franz Gratwohl*

The first one who is active in this field is the Italian conceptual artist *Cesare Pietroiusti* (b. 1956). Although he often uses banknotes as a concrete physical medium, the message he sends, in my our opinion, is more on an immaterial, abstract level, perhaps even transcendental, with a religious connotation.

After all, what happens if you swallow a banknote? That's what Pietroiusti and his fellow artist Paul Griffith did. In 2007 *visitors were invited to take part in a humorous money auction which culminated in the artists eating the banknotes of the highest bid. Upon swallowing the money, the pair then waited for the notes to be naturally evacuated. Remaining amazingly intact having undergone the digestive process, they were then displayed (...) alongside a video of the auction, before being returned to the successful bidder.*[33]

Some years later, in 2011, he did a similar performance in the studio of the Moscow artist and sculptor *Boris Orlov*, but now *effectuated by a small community of eight participants, all representing different roles in the art system and different modes of its conceptualization. At the beginning of this performance, Pietroiusti distributed among the participants the largest banknotes of the world leading currencies.*[34] The participants were the contemporary art collector and dealer *Igor Markin (10,000 Japanese Yen note)*, the independent curator *Viktor Misiano (500 euro note)*, the Museum curator *Ekaterina Zenzinova (100 Canadian dollar note)*, the philosopher *Keti Chukrov (100 US dollar note)*, the economist *Daniil Shestakov (100 Australian dollar note)*, the sociologist *Alexander Sogomonov (200 Swiss Franc note)*, the film director *Andrey Silvestrov (10,000 Russian ruble note* , and the representative of the Moscow Museum of Modern Art *Ekaterina Perventseva (50 GB pounds note)*. The performers then were supposed to chew the banknotes for ten minutes. After that Boris Orlov made a sculptural object of the pulp, being the product of this collective effort. Then the resulting art object was discussed in the group and after that the 'sculpture' was exhibited.

What a peculiar thing to do, eating and chewing banknotes, you might think. But eating money is not new! Think about the origin of money: **cattle** and **salt** for instance. Besides for food, cattle was also used as money in the old days. The Latin word **pecus** means cattle, beast or animal, and refers to money: the origin of the word pecuniary. Cattle as money belongs to the category *Commodity Money*, like salt, which is the etymological origin of our word salary. So, when the artists are eating money in the form of banknotes, they don't just eat a piece of paper, but also a kind of pecuniary commodity that refers to the origin of money.

And there's even more to it than meets the eye, and that's the religious dimension of this performance. To see the connection, look at the Eucharistic wafer: *The wafer was expressly manufactured like coin: it was pressed between wafer irons and impressed with insignia like those of coins,* Marc Shell says.[35] And: *That the manufacturing process of making the Eucharistic wafer from flour paste was often technically similar to making coins from metal ingots allowed thinkers like Nicholas of Cusa in fifteenth-century Germany to observe how the Eucharistic wafer's symbolic representation of the body of Jesus – or its actually being that body – has a numismatically iconic character.* So the Eucharistic wafer is conceptually numismatic, although *Christian thinkers were often driven to contrast the wafer with coin much as they contrasted God with the devil,* Shell says.

But the wafer is a numismatic signifier, you could say, a kind of coin, but not a banknote and it's not made of paper either. Well, yes, but that's only a difference in the material of the signifier, because the message is the same: eating money is a holy ritual. Money is a sign of the Holy Spirit and there is also a bank in His name: the Vatican *Bank of the Holy Spirit.* I quote Marc Shell again: *Monetary papers issued by the Vatican's memorably named 'Bank of the Holy Spirit' seem similarly to conjoin the Holy Spirit with the intellectual quality of the monetary token.* So, in eating money, one is eating a sign, a value sign, a value message. Because, with money the medium is the message! The signifier is the coin or the banknote and these signifiers are the bearers of the (holy) money sign.

A second artist who occupied himself with eating money, is the Swiss artist *Franz Gratwohl* (b. 1967). In 1999 he made the Video *Swallow Value,* in which the open mouth of a girl is shown who receives the host in the shape of a coin.[36] *The ritual ingestion thus becomes a critique of consumption and capitalism, while the linguistic humor of the title and the time loop of swallowing, unbearably extended in time, ironically illustrates the paradoxical relationship between use and exchange value,* it is said on the website of the *Neuer Berliner Kunstverein (n.b.k.).*[37] The focus on the paradoxical relationship between *use value* and *exchange value* here is important. Paradoxical, because the use value in this case is zero or even less than zero, as coins are not very suitable for food. But the exchange value, expressed in this video, in my view is related to the exchange value of the Eucharistic wafer, that is exchangeable into the body of Christ. But although the Swiss curator *Rayelle Niemann* in principle is referring to this artwork as *religious art*,[38] in her interpretation she gives a more secular explanation. There she says that Franz Gratwohl in this video *playfully explores the borderline between innocence and brutal power.* In her opinion the video is dealing with seduction and *the eroticism of money with its implied power* and she relates it to addiction: *greed, wanting more and more leading to uncontrollable behavior. In this video the depiction of values covers a merely material level. But furthermore ethical values are questioned with the profane image of a child receiving a coin and swallowing it. (...) Selfish and monetary pleasure is taking advantage of this weakness.*

In this first chapter I was talking about the mystery of money and searching for the soul of the (money) sign. I started with *Sebastian Siechold*, who tried to find out what money really is by sending letters with this question to European national banks. I don't know if it helped him to clear the mystery of money. By collecting money jokes he may have shown that the soul of money basically can be found in a kind of laugh.

We saw that money sometimes is used by artists and other people as a medium to send messages. As said before, the money medium for this purpose can be used or tackled in many ways: by burning, eating, cutting, folding, knitting, gluing, sculpturing, crucifying, stamping, hammering, hacking, shredding, inserting inscriptions, redecorating or revaluing the money signifiers amongst others. In this chapter I gave some examples of burning and eating money, by which the artists were sending some kind of message.

In burning artificial money and replicas of consumer goods, messages are sent to dead ancestors in China. Those messages are about wishing them the best and a prosperous life after death without shortages.

But when *The Joker* in the Batman movie was burning real money, he was sending quite a different message, namely a message of power, frightening and chaos.

Then there was the Money Burning Guy *jonone100* with his message of morality and forgiveness, referring to the ritual sacrifices of cattle which was the origin of common money.

And what was the message of the K-Foundation to burn a million pounds? Well, they didn't really know why they did it. They were depressed by the money millstone around their necks and decided to get rid of it by burning it. Why? Out of a list of 5,000 reasons to do so, after ample consideration they concluded that burning the money was a constructive thing to do, because nobody's ever done it before.

The message of the money burning act on Wall Street was of a different category. *Dread Scott* was not burning dollar bills because he wanted to deliver some holy sign, but he was sending a simple secular message: he alluded to the absurdity of a market where billions of dollars can vanish in an instant. As said, this performance fits in the number 3 of Higgs' list: protest.

The bitcoin burning of *Geraldine Juárez* I think was about number 5 of Higgs list: currency validation. With the burning of bitcoins like real money, she demonstrated that bitcoins are a kind of real money.

The message in the money burning tables at the end of the examples isn't of a religious character either. The old question asked here is about the value of money, in this case tinted paper representing the figure 50. The table gives the illusion that the face value of the bills is constantly burning: related to number 5 on the list: currency validation.

In eating money I discovered a relation to the Eucharistic wafer and the ritual ingestion of money. By eating the money signifier, the artists swallowed the holy money sign and in this way perhaps came closer to the soul of money.

In the next chapters some other forms of money treatments will pass. The question about the value of money will inevitably pass by, starting with chapter 2 on The Golden Delusion.

2

The Golden Delusion

Aurum and aura

From way back the outstanding symbol for wealth is gold. But why? Why does a bar of gold give many people an idea of wealth in preference to the same amount in banknotes? Because gold represents a material real value and a banknote doesn't? Because gold is more stable in value than banknotes? On close consideration these answers only seem to provoke more questions. For what might this 'material, real value' be and what does 'stable in value' mean? The material, real value concerns the aurum, the substance of gold. But the stability in value of the gold depends among other things on the aura, i.e. the attraction and appearance of the material. Artists who occupy themselves with money art are aware of this and use it in their artwork. This chapter is about artists who consider and incorporate gold in their art.

The Money Changer and His Wife, *Quentin Massijs*

What is the wife of the moneylender looking at? What does she see? The Flemish artist *Quentin Massijs* or *Quentin Metsys* (1464/5-1530) painted an early banker in 1514 who is weighing coins. The painting is called *The Money Changer and His Wife* which hangs in the Louvre in Paris.[39]

The painting has been chosen as an illustration on the cover of many books and stories on money and money art.

The moneylender is not checking his coins just for fun, but out of necessity because you could not fully trust money in those days. Not even gold and silver coins, because people tampered with them. They were clipping them for instance. They cut and scraped little parts of the gold coins and gathered gold dust by rubbing or sieving them and the coins also suffered wear by daily use. So clipping, sweating, wearing and monarchs melting these old coins down for new ones with a lower precious metal content always threatened the money system.

So the moneylender is checking the required weight and caliber of the coins while his wife is looking at his work. Seated next to him she is distracted from her illustrated *Book of Hours*, a devout work with prayers and psalms. She has just turned a page with a picture of the Madonna and her child. But being distracted from her devout book by filthy lucre is a fateful sign. According to the Louvre's website we are dealing with a painting with a moral message: it judges human vice and reminds the viewers of the fragility of life. The shining gold, together with the pearls (symbol of desire) and some jewels on the front of the table, have distracted the woman from her divine duties. Distracted by the Mammon, you could say.

But let me repeat the question: the banker's wife is distracted by the look of the money, but what does she see?

There may be real coins lying on the money changer's table, but their attraction isn't caused by the discs themselves (aurum, the signifier), but by what this coin material, this money body symbolizes to the money changer and his wife, so what they represent (aura, the sign). And that's wealth, power, prosperity, independence, freedom from worry, status, happiness – yes, happiness too, although that representative side of money often turns out to be a fata morgana. Hence, when looking at it in this way, such a money changer and his wife behind their table are in cloud-cuckoo land, a kind of paradise. They are imagining all kinds of things. While weighing and counting, images and promises are circulating in their minds, promises of a land of milk and honey. That's why his wife has this faraway gaze.

This gaze you may come across in a number of similar paintings: in two works by *Marinus van Reymerswaele* for instance, who lived in the same period of time (1490-1546). One is hanging in the *Alte Pinakothek* in Munich and the other in the *Koninklijk Museum voor Schone Kunsten* in Antwerp, but both represent the same as the money changer by Massijs, namely *The Banker and His Wife.* And also in these two paintings the bankers' wives are looking at the coins lying on the table with a similar faraway gaze. So what do they see? Fantasies, ideals, options, undifferentiated purchasing power, well anything you can imagine. Those coins do lie on the table, but what they symbolize is in the minds of the money changers and their wives.

Tower of Power, *Chris Burden*

Those bankers and their wives see the same things lying there as the artist ***Chris Burden*** (1946-2015) wanted to show with his ***Tower of Power*** from 1985. This pyramid-like tower, with a bit of fantasy resembling a cathedral with a gold roof, consists of 100 kilo gold with a value of more than a million dollars, composed of 100 ingots of 1 kilogram each. Surrounding the gold are tiny figures made of paper matchsticks and sewing needles, encircling the tower like worshippers. The pyramid is barely a foot tall, and it's placed on a modest marble pedestal that puts the gold below eye level.[40] Because this sculpture is so expensive, it is constantly guarded by a security guard.

Why would a museum be interested in exhibiting a piece such as *Tower of Power*? Why would an artist want to make a work of art like this? The reasons are many. Increasingly museums have been perceived to be storehouses of treasures and the public is interested and greatly influenced by published information about the monetary values of art.[41] Often museum visitors (including museum professionals, critics, art historians and artists as well) travel from label to label searching for works by the famous, the economically accredited artists. Works by lesser known artists are frequently passed by and overlooked. Galleries are rehung by curators who are necessarily well-informed about recent sales in London and New York. So part of the hype of Tower of Power is it's monetary value.

On the intertwining of art and money the art critic *Robert Hughes* wrote a piece in *The New York Review of Books*, as early as 1984, from which I quote the next excerpt:[42]

I cannot help feeling a twinge of regret – at the way in which the monetary value of museum art has been moved to the forefront of people's experience. Twenty-five years ago it was easier to appreciate works of art in their true quality: what the masterpiece, laden with fetishistic value, has lost today is a certain freedom of access – a buoyancy, an availability to the eye and to the mind. It has been invested with a spurious authority, like the façade of a bank.

This process began, for many of us, when the Metropolitan Museum spent 2.3 million on Rembrandt's painting of Aristotle Contemplating the Bust of Homer, and put a red velvet rope in front of it to distinguish it from all other Rembrandts. Simultaneously, the painting was imposed on us as an authoritative object – money talks – and withdrawn as a communicative one. It was as though not only Rembrandt and his painting, but Homer as well, and Aristotle too, had been appropriated as passive icons of status. Time magazine, for which I did not work then, unwittingly summed this up by putting the painting on the cover with a gold border around it instead of the customary red one – a gesture that helped cement Americans' unconscious identification of art with treasure. Twenty years later, the two have fused to a disconcerting degree.

One of the great influences on the way the public thinks about art and money has been the masterpiece-and-treasure show. These spectacles, loosely known as blockbusters, have been thick on the ground over the last decade. It used to be believed that, in order to get crowds, you had only to put on The Search for the Gold of the Tomb of the Mummy of Someone-or-Other and in they would come. Now museums are not quite so certain, since it appears that the people who attend blockbusters show no more loyalty to the museum afterward than the people who saw <u>*Raiders of the Lost Ark*</u> *did to the cinema in which they saw it. However, this device – The Treasures of the Vikings, The Gold of the Gorgonzolas – helped to reinforce the illusion that art was basically a kind of bullion.*

According to artist ***Chris Burden*** himself, the *Tower of Power* represents a connection between *aura* and *wealth (aurum)* and also between *beauty* and *power.* In many works by *Burden* the meaning-making role of banks and museums is emphasized. And because a work of art is usually shown in a museological setting, the *Tower of Power* is also a metaphorical reference to the power of the museum as an institution. Burden shows that a museum is not only a place where aesthetic and imaginary values are neutrally being exhibited, but also inevitably a place of evaluation and power and of inclusion and exclusion. In addition his installation refers to the link between aesthetic and social rules hidden in every work of art. Burden is also depicting in his gold Tower a connection between *money spirit* and *money body*, comparable to the abovementioned *aura* of the gold and the *capital (aurum)* it represents. For what do we actually see when looking at the Tower? Once more we see an illusion which appears to be surprisingly real. The same kind of illusion that put a spell on the money changer and his wife.

Easy, Breezy, Beautiful, *Sylvie Fleury*

The fascination for gold is also a main theme for the Swiss artist ***Sylvie Fleury*** (1961). She is known for her gilded sculptures of glamour, fashion and luxury products. Her most famous object is probably ***Easy, Breezy, Beautiful*** (2000), a gilded shopping trolley on a spinning mirrored pedestal. *It idolizes the moment of purchase while highlighting its barrenness,* Francesca Gavin writes.[43] And: *Fleury's use of the pedestal flirts with western society's structures of power, value and beauty, transforming the objects into something of worship yet creating an undercurrent of superficiality.* So, like Chris Burden's *Tower of Power* Sylvie Fleury's golden shopping trolley clearly refers to the link between aura and aurum.

Among the many other gilded objects that Fleury made, are for instance a ***golden Car Tire*** (2003) and ***golden Handcuffs*** (2003). *Although at first glance her works may seem like an affirmation of the consumer society and its values, on closer inspection a more subtle commentary on superficial* *beauty becomes apparent,* we read on the website of her gallery *Galerie Thaddaeus Ropac.*[44] *Her objects, wall pieces, pictures and installations assume an intrinsic value far exceeding the mere affirmation of brand names. Sylvie Fleury's sculptures always demonstrate detailed knowledge of the artistic aesthetics of Pop Art and Minimal Art, without her work developing into Art on Art. No artist has probably ever combined the idea of Duchamp's Ready Made with Warhol's affirmation of the consumer world in such unbiased way. In Fleury's sculptures, the profane assumes an aura of sanctity.*

Folkestone Digs, *Michael Sailstorfer*

The glitter of gold was also beautiful demonstrated by the German artist ***Michael Sailstorfer*** (1979) in 2014 when he hid thirty gold bars on the beach of the South English seaside resort Folkestone. Sailstorfer was invited to conceive a project for the "Folkestone Triennial 2014", which would respond to the particularities of the English coastal town and former port. He announced that he had buried 30 pieces of 24-carat gold under the sand of the Outer Harbour beach. This beach is open to the public, but becomes partly covered at high tide. Visitors to the beach were welcome to dig for the gold, or to watch the hunt unfold. Successful treasure-hunters were entitled to keep their gold.

Well, you can guess what happened. From the moment the artist announced that he had buried the thirty gold ingots, people rushed in and started digging. In a twinkling of the eye the whole beach looked like a ploughed sandbox. This kind of art is an example of *participation art*, in which the role of the public is an essential part of the artwork. *The desire to move viewers out of the role of passive observers and into the role of producers is one of the hallmarks of twentieth-century art,* art historian and art critic Claire Bishop says.[45]

Danaë project, *Vadim Zakharov*

Another compelling participation artwork on gold was the *Danaë project* at the Venice Biennale in 2013. The Russian Pavilion showed an installation of the Russian conceptual artist ***Vadim Zakharov*** (1959), who had been inspired by the story of *Danaë*, a myth from Greek mythology.

Danaë was the daughter of *Acrisius*, king of Argos, who was seduced by a gold rain. How did that happen? Well, Acrisius was disappointed that he had no sons to give his throne, and asked the oracle of Delphi for help. The oracle predicted that his grandson would kill him. At the time, Danaë was childless, and to keep the prophecy from coming true, *Acrisius* locked her in a brass tower until she would be too old to get children. However, *Zeus*, the king of the gods, desired her, and came to her in the form of a gold rain and impregnated her. She gave birth to a baby, which she named *Perseus*. When Acrisius found out what had happened, he was infuriated. Unwilling to provoke the wrath of the gods or the Furies by killing his offspring and grandchild, King Acrisius cast Danaë and Perseus into the sea in a wooden chest. The sea was calmed by Poseidon and, at the request of Zeus, the pair survived. They washed ashore on the island of *Seriphos*, where they were taken in by the fisherman *Dictys*, brother of the local ruler King *Polydectes*. Dictys raised Perseus to manhood. The King was charmed by Danaë, but she had no interest in him. Consequently, he agreed not to marry her only if her son would bring him the head of the *Gorgon Medusa*. Using Athena's shield, Hermes's winged sandals and Hades' helmet of invisibility, Perseus was able to evade Medusa's gaze and decapitates her. He eventually decided to return to Argos and see his grandfather, but after finding out about the prophecy, instead he went to Larissa, where athletic games were being held. By chance, an aging Acrisius was there and while Perseus was throwing the discus, the thing accidentally struck his grandfather on the head, resulting in his instant death. Thus, the prophecy was fulfilled.[46]

The gold rain in the myth of Danaë in modern times is often interpreted as an image of the corrupting power of money, but that is not necessarily true. It is also possible to conceive the story as a prefiguration of *The Immaculate Conception* of the Virgin Mary, by which Danaë can be understood as the personification of chastity.

Anyhow, *Zakharov* made an installation in Venice in which it literally rained money, in the form of coins. From a pyramid shaped roof it was raining coins through a large shower head. The female spectators were allowed to walk through the money rain with transparent umbrellas and pick up coins from the money pool on the floor. But after that they had to neatly put these coins into a bucket. When it had been filled, it was pulled up by a rope through a hole in the ceiling by the artist or his assistant and emptied into a conveyer belt (Jacob's ladder) which transported the coins upstairs again, after which the whole process was repeated.

I quote Zakharov on his installation:[47] *The installation has two points for viewing – from above and from below (in the central hall of the Pavilion a large square hole has been made in the ceiling of the lower exhibition space, and an altar rail with cushions for kneeling has been built on the upper floor, around the hole). Kneeling and looking down, we can grasp and feel that we are present at a unique process of materialization of myth. Through the huge hole in the floor, we fall into another semantic and poetic space, into which golden coins fly from a pyramid ceiling. Below we see women with umbrellas, which protect them from being struck by the coins. The lower hall can only be visited by women. This is not about sexism but merely follows the logic of the anatomical construction of the myth. What is masculine can only fall inside from above, in the form of golden rain. The lower level of the Pavilion is a 'cave womb', keeping tranquility, knowledge, and memory intact.*

Danaë paintings, *Gustav Klimt, Titian, Correggio, Rembrandt*

The myth of Danaë also inspired many painters. Amongst them were *Gustav Klimt, Titian, Correggio* and *Rembrandt.* One of the most famous Danaë paintings is the one of *Gustav Klimt* of 1907. His painting captures the image of the princess imprisoned by the king in a bronze tower, while a golden rain flows between her legs. Her face shows signs of arousal by the golden stream. *"The artist is trying to create a quintessential symbol of transcendence and divine love using Danaë as the main protagonist of his artwork,"* according to the website of **Totally History.**[48] In this work, Danaë is curled in a royal purple veil which refers to her imperial lineage. The picture is also characterized as an example of Symbolism. It is an oil on canvas painting, measures 77 x 83 cm and is in the collection of *Galerie Würthle* in Vienna.

The Venetian master *Titian* painted at least five canvasses on this mythological princess between 1540 and 1570. The version from 1544 was called *Danaë with Eros* (120 x 172 cm) and is in the collection of the *National Museum of Capodimonte (Museo di Capodimonte)* in Naples. Other works are to be found in the *Hermitage Museum* in Saint Petersburg (from the period 1553-54) and the *Kunsthistorisches Museum* in Vienna (1564).

Rembrandt's painting Danaë (185 x 203 cm) from 1636 resides in the *Hermitage Museum* in St. Petersburg, Russia, since the 18th century. It is a life-sized depiction of the princess. The artist's wife Saskia was the original model for Danaë, but Rembrandt later changed the figure's face to that of his mistress Geertje Dircx.

My last example of Danaë paintings is a work by the Italian Renaissance artist Correggio. *Antonio da Correggio* (1489-1534) painted his Danaë around 1531 and is now housed in the *Galleria Borghese* in Rome. The scene is set in an interior draped with rich and suitably folded hangings, framing a window opening onto the landscape, as if to "unveil" the union.[49] The maiden is reclining on a bed of classical design ornamented with knobs. Nearby Eros, as an intercessor between Zeus and the princess, and representing divine desire, helps her to hold the sheet, so as not to lose the golden seed.

Annunciation, *Simone Martini*

Related to the portrayals of the myth of Danaë to my opinion is the painting of the *Annunciation* by *Simone Martini* and his brother-in-law *Lippo Menni* from around 1333. It was made for the altar of Sant'Ansano in the Cathedral of Siena. The difference with Danaë is that the fertilization in the Annunciation is effected by the ear through the Word of God, but those words in this case are also Golden Words!

On the website of the Uffizi Museum in Florence you can read this explanation about the *Annunciation* by

Simone Martini: *The Archangel has just touched ground in front of the Virgin as shown by his unfold wings and his swirling mantle. The scene seems a* ***theatrical performance,*** *as stressed by the comic strip like sentence in the middle of the composition with the greeting of the angel. The Virgin is portrayed almost surprised and frightened by the sudden appearance. Her movement, so prim and elegant, adds a certain effect of sophistication to the work. The altarpiece has a gold background, so bound to tradition, and still very much in demand for the depictions of sacred stories. The artist adhered therefore to what customers required, but they used to insert some details that could make the composition more realistic. For this purpose Simone Martini included some delightful details in the main scene as the marble floor, the mantle of the Archangel, the pot of lilies, the half-closed book of Mary and her throne, all of which suggest a real space, otherwise penalized by the gold background. The garments of the four characters take shape thanks to the snaky and decorative line typical of Sienese school. The painting is then fully Sienese for the beauty and the gentleness of lines and colors, just in opposition to Florentine style, more related to the volume and the shape.*[50]

So far I presented some artists who were fascinated by the aurum and aura of gold. However, this aura can be delusive. Money artists recognize this and use it in their works, as shown before in some of the preceding examples.

Von Explosionen zu Ikonen, *Alicja Kwade*
Another important and interesting exponent of this group of artists is *Alicja Kwade,* a conceptual artist, born in Poland (1979) and working in Berlin. In 2008 she made an installation called *Von Explosionen zu Ikonen*, consisting of a pile of 666 gilded coal briquettes of the Union firm. It was a visualization of the "black gold", which had been the fuel for the economic engine for years. But this fuel was at the end of its heyday. Most mines had been closed down and present-day energy supply mainly comes from oil, gas, nuclear power and more and more sustainable energy sources like wind and sun. Hence, coal has become an old-fashioned energy source, as obsolete as the almost *lächerlich altertümliche Goldbegehren* as the artist calls it. With the additional printing of the word *Rekord* on her gilded briquettes *Alicja Kwade* shows our value structures to the point of absurdity. By treating coal, gold and money as equals, the artist dethrones gold of its holy value, which makes clear how randomly a foundation of value is chosen. Anything can be proclaimed a value-icon. The title of the artwork refers to this: *Von Explosionen zu Ikonen.* By gilding the briquettes and piling up 666 of them, the fuel, the 'explosion-product' gets the aura of an almost holy/diabolic icon.

How do we define value? is the opening question in an article on *Alicja Kwade* on the website of *modern edition.com.*[51] *In what way does a material's properties dictate assumptions regarding its identity and worth? (...) Kwade herself has emphasized that (...) All my materials are so loaded with symbolic meaning. (...) Pointing out* ***the arbitrary way in which we structure our world and how we determine what is valuable and what is not,*** *Kwade contrasts the lowly status of coal – a provider of essential heat and electric power – with (...)* ***gold, that is not a very useful material, but something we abstractly decided to be something special, just because it's yellow and shiny.*** In Kwade's eyes the preferential hierarchies ascribed to certain materials seem illogical or even absurd. Why should gold be of more value than lead or iron? *By overturning our common understanding of material properties, such works simultaneously undermine teleology's which, like the preference for gold over coal, ultimately dictate a particular view of the world.*

Soil-erg, *Claire Pentecost*

This view is also shared by the American artist Claire Pentecost (1956), who exhibited her installation **Soil-erg** at the art manifestation *Documenta 13* in the Ottoneum Kassel in 2012. It consists among others of soup plate-sized coins and piles of ingots resembling gold ingots, but instead made of earth and compost. Large bank note-like drawings 'painted' in earth and compost too, were hanging on the wall. With this installation Pentecost meant to offer an alternative for the privileged dominion of gold and dollar. That's why she made all these money symbols, or should we say symbols of economic power, from earth and natural compost. This soil is of vital importance and has all the necessary qualities a currency should have in future according to her. Sound soil and seeds are endangered from all sides nowadays in becoming privatized and poisoned by pesticides, fertilizer and other chemicals. Pentecost encourages people to face these facts and to start the production of sound soil themselves by learning how to compost. In view of this she added an 'auditory sculpture', in which a section of fertile soil is shown behind glass to the spectators, who can meanwhile listen to amplified sounds of worms productively turning up the soil.

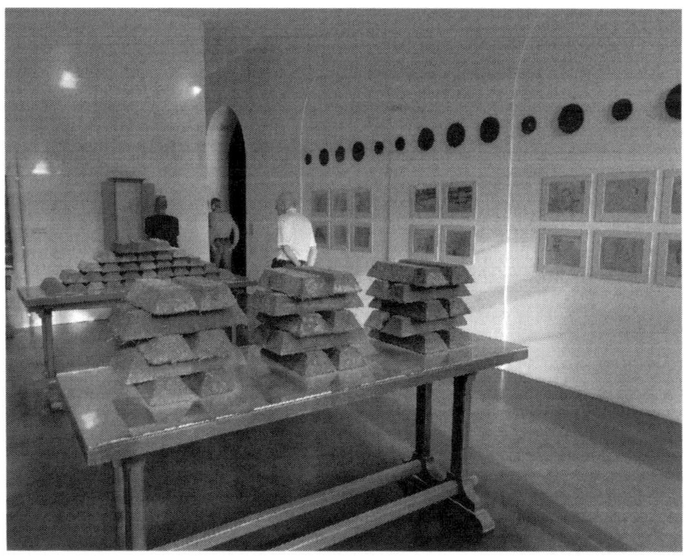

Claire Pentecost, Soil-Erg 2012, Documenta 13, Kassel

(Photo by Reinold Widemann)

By this artwork Claire Pentecost has returned the idea of money and value circulating in our minds to the place where in her view this entire value originates from: the earth. Our earth eventually delivers all our food and all our raw materials, and therefore we have to be careful with it.

But in the meantime we have to deal with the dictatorship of gold as the most valuable material. Gold on top of the value hierarchy dictates a particular view of the world – illogical and absurd, according to Alicja Kwade and Claire Pentecost. For a long time in history people have chosen gold as the superior foundation of money. And that's ridiculous, because we can choose anything we like as the basis of money. Gold isn't money, silver isn't money and paper isn't money, but money can be of gold, silver or paper. Or any product whatsoever. Or even no product at all, for money is just based on an agreement, on credit, an IOU. The material foundation is of no real importance for the money system, because money is a function, an abstract function. The chosen money matter is just a vehicle or instrument with which we pursue this function. But it took a while in history before most people understood this concept of that function of money – or: re-understood, we might rather say, as originally money was nothing but a debt arrangement, for which at the most a mnemonic device was needed, like a tally stick.

Anyway, the dictatorship of gold as foundation of money has long persevered and this belief is still persistent among the gold fetishists. But gold can be a devastating footing of money if there is not enough of it. Why? Because in that case, when demand for gold exceeds supply, the price of gold is rising and so the money linked to it will become more expensive too. And more expensive money means lower prices for goods and services. So, not inflation, but deflation. But isn't that great, lower prices for our daily shopping, you could ask. No, that isn't great, that's very bad, because deflation pushes people out of their jobs.

An historic example of this evil of gold dictatorship took place around 1870 in America. It was caused by the insufficient increase of the gold supply in comparison to the real national product, so there wasn't enough money (gold) in circulation compared to the goods and service trade. It made gold more expensive, which caused the prices to decrease. Between 1869 and 1879 for example the American money supply increased with merely 2.6 percent per year, while the production increased with 5.0 percent per year. This scarcity of money led to deflation. According to the supporters of the bimetallic standard this scarcity of money could easily be met when beside gold, silver was allowed to be used as money too. But this had been made impossible by the ***Crime of 1873***. This 'Crime of 1873' was the demonetization of silver by the *'Coinage Act of 1873'*. As a result the double or bimetallic standard, which had existed for nearly a century, was put out of action. This standard had been established in 1792 under Alexander Hamilton and functioned fairly well. In practice this double standard actually turned out to be a single standard of sometimes gold and sometimes silver owing to Gresham's Law,[52] but it did make it possible to meet deficits of gold or silver. This flexibility disappeared from the system by choosing the single gold standard – from that moment onwards the economy was nailed to the "Cross of Gold".

The Cross of Gold, *Victor Dubreuil*

The 19th century *trompe l'oeil* master *Victor Dubreuil* (ca. 1840-1908) made a classic money painting of this devilish cross. Trompe l'oeil painting is a "fool the eye" technique, in this case still life paintings of bills and coins in such detail that viewers were tempted to pluck them of the canvas. Dubreuil remains a rather shadowy figure in the history of trompe l'oeil still life painting, since little of his biography has been traced. Although his works are well known and included in prominent private museum collections, his life has remained mystery.[53] He may have been the son of a French couple, who emigrated to New York around 1847. He had several occupations: he was a soldier, socialist, artist, involved in banking and he owned a short-lived newspaper. And he was obsessed with money.

"You shall not crucify mankind on a cross of gold!" presidential candidate William Jennings Bryan said 1896 in a speech against the gold standard. William Poundstone

writes about the Cross of Gold in a blog: *"Dubreuil's painting is indeed a crucifixion. Check out the abstract, horizontally banded background. The greenbacks are pinned to a support and cast shadows on it. What is the support? It is difficult to rationalize as a wall or letter rack. It looks, for all the world, like a $ 70 million Rothko,"*[54] The painting is an oil on canvas, ca. 36 x 31 cm, and is now in the Crystal Bridges Museum of American Art in Bentonville, Arkansas.

We will come across more beautiful examples of trompe l'oeil money art in chapter 4.

Art for Money – Money for Art, *Leroy Brothers*
Belgian brothers *Nicolas* (1979), *Gilles* (1978) and *Gregory* (1975) are the creative minds behind the Art Collective *Leroy Brothers*. In 2012 they made a money art installation showing three characters in the economical crisis. The first character we see is a silver mole crawling out of a molehill of gold coins, leaving behind a trace of gold coins. The gold coins do not consist of existing coins, but were especially designed for the installation by the Leroy Brothers. This mole is the **Gold-digger**, *a metaphor for those who travel to emerging countries to seek fortune.*[55] In another heap of gold a squirrel is provisioning gold coins in his home, a trunk of a tree. The squirrel represents the **Saver**. Thirdly, there is the **Lavish Spender**, represented by a piggy bank that broke itself in order to be able to consume more. This broken

piggy bank stands for *the thousands of households putting themselves in debt to acquire materialistic products.* According to the Leroy Brothers, the three characters represent a contemporary version of *the fables of de la Fontaine.*

Bright Future Horizons, *Anna Ihle*

Nearly every artist struggles to fund their art practice, as well as their living expenses, DJ Panning writes on the *Creators* site.[56] Norwegian artist *Anna Ihle* (1984) was one of those artists and decided to show this hustle to the world in an artwork called ***Bright Future Horizons*** (2016). With a group of fellow-sufferers from the art world, she went for gold panning in Savanger, the oil capital of Norway. All her fellow gold miners came from Stavanger, but didn't know each other before the trip. (Besides Anna Ihle this gold crew consisted of Uma Feed, Espen Birkedal, Jens Borge and Siri Borge.) She documented the results in documentary shorts, work journals, motivational posters, mining tools and maps. This documentation also features World War II-era images of *jolly, happy gold-digging people* from the private archive of the landowner who owns the cabin where the crew was based.

Did the group find gold? *I've learned that gold diggers don't answer that question,* Ihle replied, but finding gold (the aurum) was not the real purpose of this work. She wanted to *poke at (…) motivational forces that cause many of us to work too hard. How can they be identified? Where are they to be found? Which ones are to be kept, and which ones are fake?* With this performance Anna Ihle also called for attention to artist's irregular sources of income.

She exhibited her project in the form of a video installation, 5 video loops, archival material and posters and ready-mades, but I don't think she or someone else from her group got rich through this panning for gold. Perhaps we could conclude that the artistic aura that supposedly hangs around artists doesn't often pay in the form of aurum, i.e. real money.

3

Evergreen?

Songs of love and hate

Dollar Bills and Dollar Signs, *Andy Warhol*

Was Andy Warhol (1928-1987) in love with the dollar? Yes, he was obsessed with money! He loved to make it, loved to paint it, and he loved to spend it: *Cash. I just am not happy when I don't have it. The minute I have it I have to spend it. And I just buy STUPID THINGS.*[57] Warhol grew up without much of it in Depression-era Pittsburgh. From an early age, he developed an obsession with money that would accompany him throughout his life even when he reached the level of absolute material security.[58] His diaries reveal how meticulously he noted each cab fare and ticket price until his death in 1987. He openly indulged accumulating and amassing random things, up to the point that his apartment was barely accessible.

The dollar first appeared in Warhol's artwork in the early 1960's. In that time he was looking for a way to make his name in the New York art world and asked his friends for suggestions about what to paint.[59] Warhol said: *Finally, one old lady friend asked the right question: Well, what do you love most? That's how I started painting money.* The first picture he made was a hand-painted dollar bill canvas, *One*

Dollar Bill (Silver Certificate) from 1962. Warhol painted it based on a photograph of currency. This dollar bill painting is the only one he painted by hand before hitting on his silk-screen technique. Screen printing is a method of reproducing images by using a finely-woven mesh of 'silk-screen' to support an ink-blocking stencil. In this technique he drew in ink on acetate, creating images of dollar bills that he then duplicated a total of 200 times in his famous *200 One Dollar Bills* from 1962[60] (in 1986 bought by an art collector for $ 385,000 and sold in 2009 at Sotheby's for $ 43.8 million). In the same year 1962 he also made a similar multiple: *192 One Dollar Bills.*

Returning to the subject in 1981, Warhol isolated the symbol denoting dollars, and made it the focus of his artwork: the *Dollar Sign*. The dollar sign emerges as a modern-day symbol of secular worship in a capitalist society driven by financial wealth and superficial appearances. *Arthur C. Danto* pointed out that, within the constraints of the archetypical form of the dollar symbol *he used and combined colors in the same way in which he made his portraits as if these were portraits, so to speak, of the dollar sign – about the dollar sign as physiognomic, and abstracted from the numerical expressions that it transforms into dollar amounts.*[61]

The Dollar Sign paintings by Andy Warhol contain a source image that was created by himself. So this image had not been appropriated from the mass media or reproduced from a photograph, but was actually hand-drawn. The separate Dollar Signs are part of Dollar Sign series, screen prints in vibrant hues and rhythmic repetition of the single $ motif. An example is the *Dollar Sign 275* as part of a series from 1982, an ultimate manifestation of Warhol's love affair with money. He once said: *I like money on the wall,* and the Dollar Sign Series was his way of using his iconic imagery to achieve that. The series is comprised of multiple variations of dollar sign screen prints on Lenox Museum Board.

Warhol's paintings have become icons of popular culture and achieved an unparalleled level of success that allowed him to declare: *Big-time art is big-time money.* Money as art and art as money, you might say.

Green Dollar Sign on Malevich's Suprematism,
Alexander Brener[62]

In 1997 Russian performance artist *Alexander Brener* (1957, Alma-Ata) walked into the *Stedelijk Museum* of Modern Art in Amsterdam. He went straight to the room where *Kazimir Malewich* famous work of art *Suprematism* was exhibited, took a canister of green aerosol paint out of a concealing coat pocket and sprayed a dollar symbol with two vertical lines on Malevich's painting. Immediately after being apprehended by security guards, he loudly proclaimed that what he had done was performance art and a dialogue with Malevich about corruption in the commercial art world. Malevich's masterpiece valued $ 7.5 million at that time and dropped to $ 5 million in the wake of this 'modification'. A modification indeed, as Brener called it, not an act of vandalism!

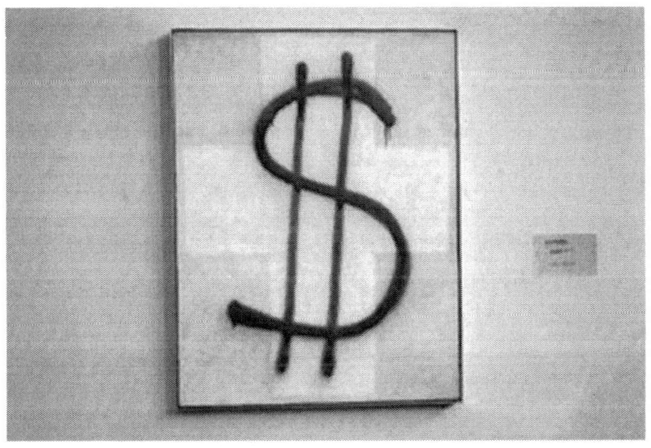

Malevich's Suprematism after Brener's modification.

As opposed to other historical cases of vandalism against art, Brener was not provoked by the work of art itself, only by the physical and economic context in which it was located. In fact Brener identified with Malevich and wanted to blend his paint with the artist's. Spray-painting the work of art was Brener's way of taking it seriously. From that point of view you might say that the synthesis of Malevich and Brener had created something new, that had critics lauded with approval and might have required protection as a new art object entirely.[63] Some critics commented on how it enhanced the painting with a new layer of significance. So in this case Brener perhaps had better be referred to as a "quality vandal" like *Banksy*, whose street art is now often *shielded by Plexiglas and boasts a wooden nameplate.*[64]

One Billion Dollar (Most Expensive Artwork Ever), *Michael Marcovici*

Another artist who depicted his fascination or awe for the dollar was the Austrian *Michael Marcovici* (1969, Vienna). In 2009 he stacked altogether 10 million 100 USD notes on 12 standard pallets: *One Billion Dollar*, the most expensive piece of art ever made, the artist claimed. Around that time *Damien Hirst* just got trumped as the most valuable living artist. His skull *For the Love of God* was covered in diamonds with a value of around $ 100 million. Does this mean that by creating his *One Billion Dollar* work Marcovici overtook the first place and became the most valuable living artist at that moment? That would perhaps be the case if his work had been sold, but in this case it was not about the selling price but the inherent or intrinsic value of the artwork. And was it real money he stacked on the pallets? I'll tell you in a minute.

The artist wanted *to draw attention to the part that value and pricing plays in art and everything else.* In an explanation he wrote that this artwork *is not so much about what you see, but what you could do or not do with the money.* You can read this as a reference to the dualism between money body and money spirit, in which it's all about this spirit, about the imagination of material and immaterial wealth these pallets loaded with money evoke.

In physically realizing this project, the artist had some difficulties getting all the money together, because *actually no bank has this amount of cash, there are several cash handling facilities where the old money gets exchanged to new notes and where money from large retailers is handled, places like those have sufficient of cash for such an action, the problem is just that it is expensive to do it because timing is very tight already in these places (and security too).*[65] So the original plan to exhibit real money failed because of exorbitant high interest rates for providing the money and the demanded securities. Who would deliver him the money for *One Billion Dollar* then? Maybe a government? Or a fabulously wealthy art friend? It turned out nobody did.

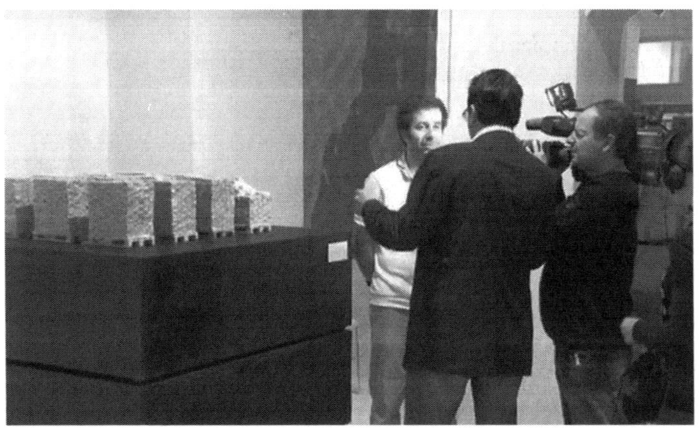

Michael Marcovici and his *One Billion Dollar*.

How did the artist solve this problem? Well, he made a small scale model. The art piece isn't real money at all, but a sculpture with the proportion 1 : 6.

100,000 Dollar Wall, *Hans – Peter Feldmann*

Conceptual artist *Hans – Peter Feldmann*, (1941, Düsseldorf) displayed a *100,000 Dollar – Wall* in the Guggenheim Museum in New York in 2011. He was the winner of the $100,000 Hugo Boss Prize 2010, and had chosen to post 100,000 older, pre-circulated one dollar US bills on the wall of the museum. He had the bills individually fixed on the walls and pillars with single finishing nails. He said: *I began making art in the '50's. At that time there was no money in the art world. So for me 100,000 USD is very special. It's incredible really, and I would like to show the quantity of it.*[66] When people entered the room, their noses were filled with a pervasive, musty smell of thousands of used dollar bills, some stained or wrinkled, others crossed with stay red or blue or black marks.[67] *It reeks of culture,* a visitor joked.[68]

The value of money is a mass delusion, yet every abstract swell and ebb of its worth has some real effect chronicled in the daily news, art critic *Maika Pollack* wrote in *The Observer.*[69] We shouldn't try to read anything into this artwork, Feldmann said, for it was just what it showed: *Money = Art.* He had received the money shortly before as winner of the *Hugo Boss Prize,* a biennial prize since 1996.

According to Guggenheim curator Katherine Brinson, Feldmann's *$100,000* reminds gallery-goers that dollar bills, like artworks, have no inherent worth beyond what society invests in them. However, the piece, she added, is actually less about the symbolism of capitalist excess than it is about the mass-produced image.[70]

So Money = Art or Art = Money, a kind of economic cycle, in this case a cycle of two countercyclical types of money. A sort of congruency. Because if Feldmann assumes that money is a form of art, and if you turn it around, we actually speak of two kinds of currency traded in a special type of financial market, and this market is the currency market. In the currency market different currencies are being exchanged, like dollars for Euros, and according to *Hans – Peter Feldmann* art should be seen as a currency. I will come back to this statement extensively in chapter 4, where I'll discuss that Art = Money.

Money Shark and a whitewashed mural with Dollar Coffins, *Blu*

Blu is an Italian street artist, whose huge murals have appeared around the world. His work dramatizes money's power to transform human agency and possibility. In a well-known piece from 2010 for instance, Blu covered a tapering wall in Barcelona in the image of a massive shark composed of dollar bills. It was his grim commentary on the paroxysms of austerity forced on Spain as a result of global financial meltdown after the financial crisis of 2008. The term 'money shark' refers to 'loan shark', which is a person or a body who offers loans at extremely high interest rates such as payday or title loans. They sometimes enforce repayment by blackmail or threats of violence. Loan sharks are illegal lenders who often target low income and desperate families. In the case of Spain after 2008 this country was in some ways comparable to such a 'desperate family' with low income en huge debts, that had to be repaid. In that time Spain had a low credit rating and therefore had to pay relative high interest rates for their public loans.

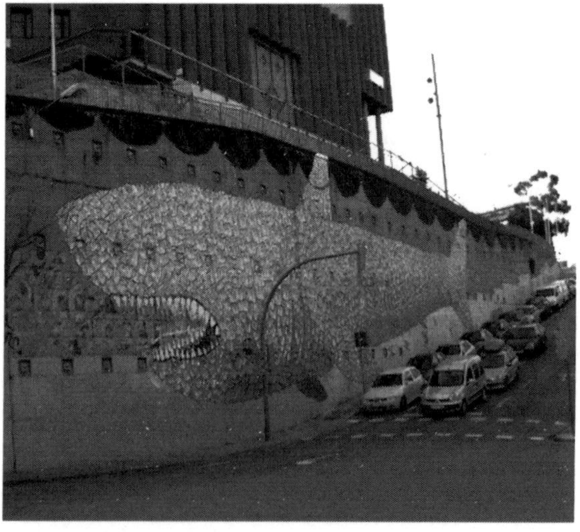

Blu's *Money Shark* in Barcelona, 2010.

Another famous money artwork Blu painted, was the mural of wooden coffins draped in American dollar bills he created also in 2010 on the side of a satellite location of the Museum of Contemporary Art in Los Angeles. The museum is located near-by a war memorial and Blu made his mural in a fashion reminiscent of the propaganda and rituals of military funerals. So I think you can guess what happened to it.

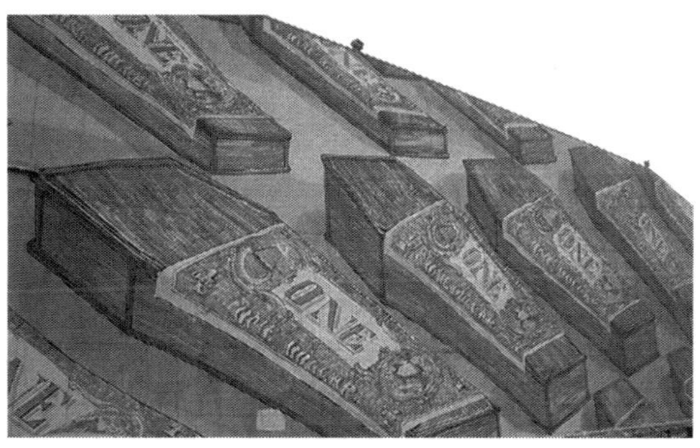

Blu, *mural of coffins with dollar bills* on the MOCA, 2010.

The museum had the piece whitewashed within 24 hours:

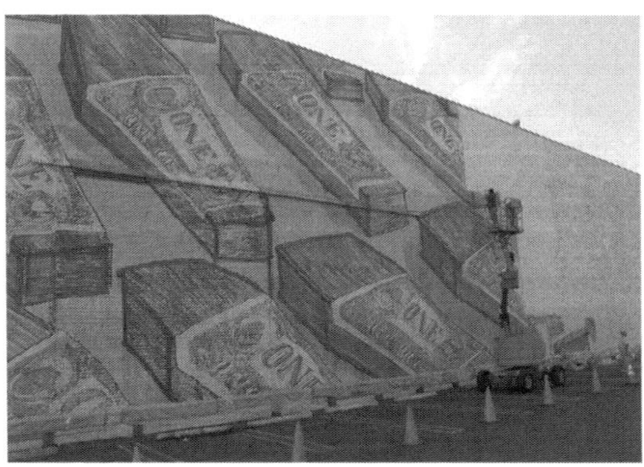

Whitewashing the mural of Blu on the side of the MOCA.

Dollar skulls, *Scott Campbell*

After abandoning a career as a biochemist, *Scott Campbell* (1977) began tattooing. He did not complete his degree as a biochemist at the University of Texas and opened a tattoo shop in Brooklyn, which client list includes New York's art and design elite and a long range of other celebrities. Aside from his tattoo work, he is also famous for laser-cutting designs into stacks of U.S. one dollar bills, a series he called **One Dollar Art**. When producing this series, Campbell sourced a great amount of uncut sheets of dollars directly from the United States Mint. He used these dollar sheets to create sculpture-like pieces with a sunken relief effect.

One of these sculptures is an intricate 3D skull out of a 2 x 2 foot (about 60 cm^2) cube of money. The skull is an image familiar in the world of tattoo, but using the technique of layered construction creates a solid three-dimensional object of the sheets of currency. This is an effective way to generate 3D forms, as it takes advantage of the precision enabled by laser cutting. The resulting topographical layers create a distinctive visual texture. In this way the three dimensional skull was carved-out. From the uncut sheets of one dollar bills totaling $11,000, he made this cube in which a spooky skull is carved out, called *Pièce de Résistance*. It alludes to mortality, yet is sculpted from the currency with which we trade our time and energy.[71]

The dollar skull raises issues of how arbitrary money can seem. By placing this iconic form into a dead-man's chest made out of $11,000 in real, legal currency, the value of money is brought into question as we reconsider how much the items that we buy are really worth.

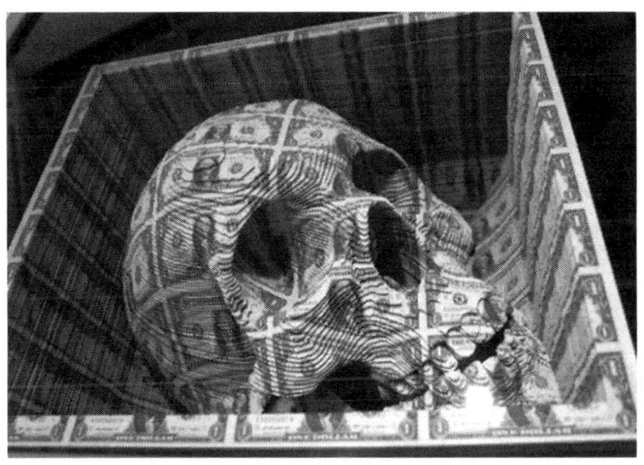

Scott Campbell, Money Skull "Pièce de Résistance".

His *Pièce de Résistance* is not the only skull he made. They all could be read as metaphors that add to the ongoing dialogue concerning the sensitive relationship between art and capitalism and how they both fit into the contemporary art scene today.[72]

Weapons and Dollars, ***Justine Smith***

As an artist *Justine Smith* (1971, Somerset) is interested in the concept of money, and how it touches almost every aspect of our lives.[73] Paper has always been a primary material in her work. Through her collages and sculptures she examines our relationship with money in a political, moral and social sense. Her money artwork is concerned with the concept of money and how it touches almost every aspect of our lives.[74] According to her website *she is interested in money as a conduit of power and also in the value systems with which we surround it.*[75] Although a banknote is just a piece of paper, it is the value with which we mentally associate it that makes it so valuable.

Focusing on the concept of money and its impact on civilization, she also exploits the physical beauty of bank notes in her money art. So not only political and social reflections are a hallmark of Justine's work, but equally, so is the thought that goes into the color and shape of the pieces. She is keen for those who design and make banknotes to be seen as artists themselves. Especially *Arab notes are beautiful,* she says. For her artwork she only uses new and uncirculated money.

The message in her *Weapons* series is *'that money can buy power and that power can be misused.'*[76] In this connection currency can be seen as an instrument of war and a conduit of power. The money art weapons she made are hand grenades, revolvers and guns.[77] Examples of her grenades are *Collateral Damage* (2007, made from one dollar bills), the *Lincoln Grenade* (*Blow,* 2014) and the grenade with a Mao decoration *Inheritance (Boom*, 2012), sculptured out of Chinese Yuan notes. She also made some revolvers, like a S & W (Smith & Wesson) 645, *Instruments of State* (2009) made of Myanmar Kyats, and one called *Judgment* or *The*

Judge (2011). A famous money rifle of her is the one made of dollar notes: *M16, Absolute PowerII* (2005).

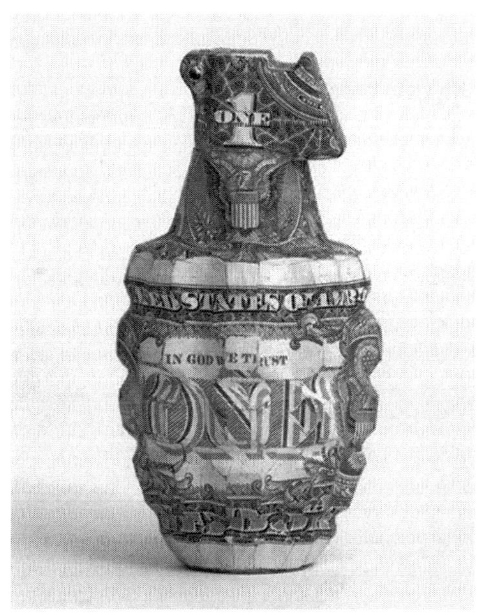

Justine Smith, *Collateral Damage* (2007).

(*Image courtesy of the artist*)

The money weapons Justine Smith created are only part of her money artwork. She also made beautiful dollar signs, like the *Holy Trinity* from 2007, three big dollar signs made of US Quarter dollars (sprayed wood, rope light), and the symbolic *Deification* (sprayed wood, rope light), also made of US Quarter dollars and from 2007.[78] And that's not all. What else can an artist create out of money? Almost anything. Justine Smith made money dogs, money flowers, money wall paper, her own version of the 'House of Cards', and last but not least an impressive range of big money maps, of which I'll tell you more in chapter 5.[79]

Money collages

Modern mediation has made collage a primary player in the contemporary conscious, Mark Wagner (1976, Wisconsin) writes in his zine *Love me tender, No 1*: **Look Sharp...** *The Philosophy and Practice of* **Collage.**[80] In his zine he finds an interesting connection between "the very essence of collage" and the phases in Hegelian dialectic: *Thesis, Antithesis, Synthesis.* The thesis corresponds to the *selection of a source material* to use for the collage (printed matter, photograph, etc.); the antithesis is the *destruction of this material* and the synthesis is the re-contextualization of *these things that have been taken apart, forming them into a new whole. (...) Concisely put, the phases are "Selection, Dissection, and Connection.*

Currency Collages, *Mark Wagner*

Mark Wagner himself destroys thousands of dollar bills yearly to create intricate currency collages. In these works he pointedly and playfully explores the intersection of wealth, power, value, and American identity.[81] His *audacious (and unlawful) destruction of this revered icon of American commerce is checked only by his virtuoso material manipulation, which renders what you will... portraits, plant life, fantasti-*

cal beasts, or allegorical scenes recasting George Washington in every roll.[82] George Washington, whose portrait graces the one dollar bill, figures prominently in many collages, chopping down his infamous cherry tree, strolling through a garden reading a newspaper, or snacking on a dollar bill. Others depict fantastical creatures and scenes, such as an island teeming with biomorphic vegetation that sits atop waves of dollar bills, or recreate iconic works like Grant Wood's *American Gothic* (1930). In addition to showcasing the uncanny precision for which Wagner is known, *the collages express poignant criticism of our addiction to money.*[83]

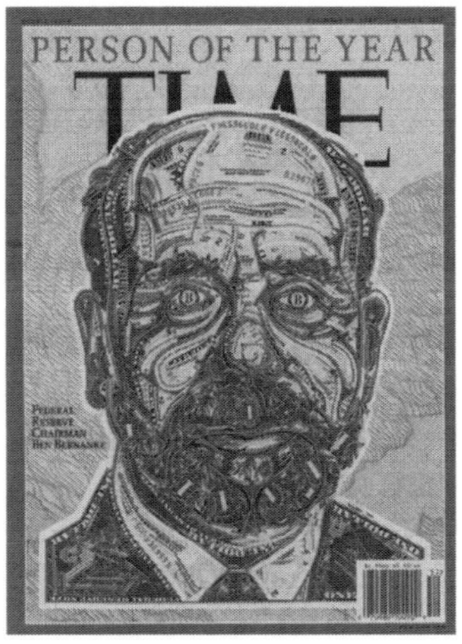

Mark Wagner, *Bernanke Time* (2010)

(Image courtesy of the artist)

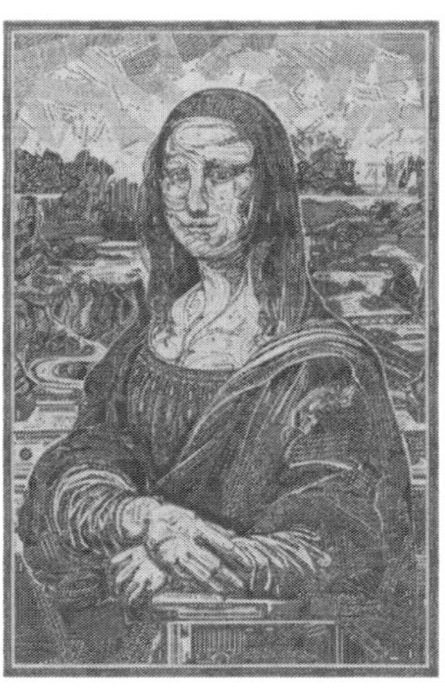

Mark Wagner, *Money Lisa*,

(Image courtesy of the artist)

Among the many currency collages Wagner made, are also the **Money Lisa**, a beautiful dollar collage portrait of the famous Lady with her mysterious smile, and the portrait of former Federal Reserve Chairman Ben Bernanke on the cover of *Time Magazine* from 2010: the **Bernanke Time**.

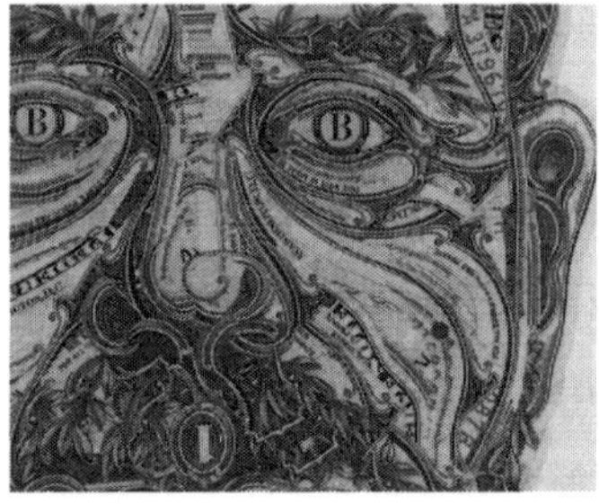
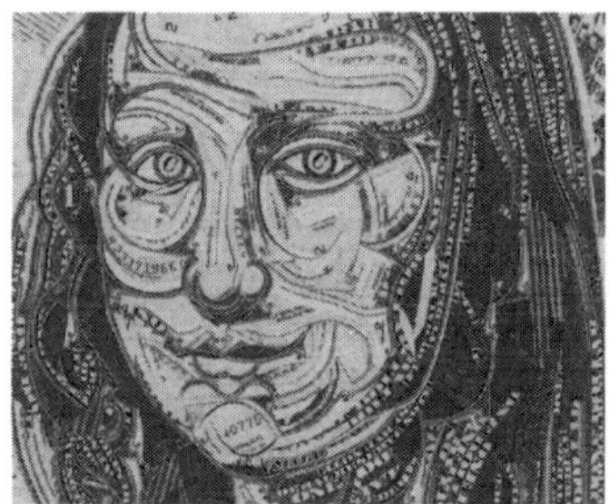

A closer look at Money Lisa and Bernanke Time.

(Image courtesy of the artist)

The dollar bill is the most ubiquitous piece of paper in the United States, said Wagner.[84] *We handle it and use it every day, but we don't stop and look at it every day. Everyone worries about money, everyone has issues with money – it's a better representation of America and Americana than even the flag. There's a lot wrapped up in that little piece of paper.* He speaks of the dollar bill as a ripe material: *intaglio printed on sturdy linen rock, covered in decorative filigree, and steeped in symbolism and concept.* Wagner tends toward meticulous assembly of his artworks. He starts cutting bills into strips, bends them, twists them, and builds them into things one at the time. You can watch him cutting and gluing on vimeo.[85]

He frequently received questions about his work, such as *Is that real money?, Isn't that illegal?, How much money went into that?, How long did that take?* and *Why money?*

If you want to know how he answered these frequently asked questions, see his Art Blog under 'F.A.Q. by MARK WAGNER.'[86]

Currency Collages, *C.K. Wilde*

Cutting up money is a disruption of the narrative of power, C.K. Wilde has written. His currency collages take on myths, legends, and icons of art history. *Christopher Karl Wilde* (1972, Madison) lived for 13 years in New York, where he lectured at NYU, and has taught Collage and Book Arts at *The Pratt Institute, The Cooper Union,* and *The Center for the Book Arts.* After that he moved to Los Angeles. His artwork can be found in over 70 collections worldwide, including *The Metropolitan Museum of Art,* and *MoMA.* His handmade books are in various public collections such as the *Bibliotecha Alexandrina* in Egypt, and the *Victoria and Albert Museum Library* in London. Wilde uses money from around the world with its broad palette of colors and designs as well as for the associations with value and might.

In 2014 he said: *My fetishization of paper money comes from my childhood. I traveled to Europe often to visit my relatives. When I returned, I often still had money from the places where I traveled. An attempt to buy candy with Deutsche Marks in the U.S. brought into sharp relief the inherent contradictions of nationalism and international travel. Are we not one people on our one planet? I thought. Why is this money powerful only in one context, useless in another?*[87]

Wilde painstakingly cuts various shapes out of the paper money to form collages with economic and political undertones and overlays. The relationship between art and commerce is another theme that cannot be avoided when an artist cuts and pastes with money. His images are based on found images, such as New York cityscapes, iconic paintings like Jacques-Louis David's *Napoleon Crossing the Alps* (1801-1805), re-imagined scenes from mythology, and of American slavery, and antique maps.[88] The work also engages contemporary global issues ranging from the politics of war to food supply. Wilde's work is driven by the image and symbolism of money as the ultimate representation of power.[89] He sometimes collaborates with his fellow currency collagist Mark Wagner who I discussed before.

Moneygami

Moneygami is origami made from currency. It is a portmanteau word that arose from the words **money** and **origami**. It refers to shaping paper currency into pieces of art. Origami is the traditional Japanese art of paper folding into various styles and shapes. The word comes from Japanese, meaning to fold (*oru*) paper (*kami*). Therefore the correct name of this kind of money would have made more sense if it had been *orimoney*. The goal of Moneygami is to create a representation of an object using geometric folds and crease patterns preferably without gluing or cutting the paper, and using only one or two banknotes. The concept has been popularized by artists such as the Swiss Moneygami master *Sipho Mabona*, Japanese pop artist *Yosuke Hasegawa*, and Hawaiian based *Won Park*.

According to *Michael LaFosse* and *Richard Alexander* from the Origami Studio in Havermill (USA)[90] the US dollar bill is a popular format because it is readily affordable, rich with intricate and artful engravings, and it is permanently printed on wonderfully strong, crisp stock. This medium stands up well to heavy folding and is particularly suited to wet-folding and the artful shaping that wet-folding affords. The dollar bill's rich tapestry of whorls, leaves, letters, and even an eye, are all elements that can be incorporated into the design of the money fold.

Moneygami with dollars: The Plague, *Sipho Mabona*[91]

A swarm of locusts hit the Japanese American National Museum in Los Angeles in 2012: **The Plague**. But this plague were no ordinary insects, but a sea of dollar bill locusts, caught in flight across one room of the exhibition. The folded dollar locusts were an installation by the Swiss origami artist *Sipho Mabona* (1980), called **The Plague**. The giant origami locusts, made of uncut squares of US currency sheets, possess a strange threatening kind of beauty and are ready to devour anything and everything that stands in their way.[92] Each of the locusts was made by meticulously folding the uncut dollar bills, without scissors, glue or adhesive. Mabona fashioned the rectangular specimens into detailed insects, complete with spanning wings, extended legs and antennae.

Sipho Mabona was five years old when he folded his first airplane, but ran out of designs for the planes by the time he was 15 and turned to other inspirations. One of these inspirations is money. *Money is our prime signifier of both ambition and perdition,* he said.[93] *Money has gone from being an elementary medium of exchange to being a means of exploitation: a colossal cloud of hot money (in the shape of incomprehensible financial instruments) buzzes above the global economy almost like a biblical swarm of locusts. Thus money is our bane. Yet money per se, when one looks at something as plain as a one-dollar-bill, always retains its basic ability to function as a pragmatic unit of account for goods & services. Therefore money is also a blessing.*

Mabona is intrigued by the concept of transformation, raising ethical questions about the use of money and power. He chose to tackle the issue of money and the duality of its symbolization of both ambition and damnation as the cause of joy and pain. With **The Plague** he compared the world's sometimes crumbling economy to the biblical legend of the locusts swarm. Was it a pessimistic installation? No, the artist stated, because far from being pessimistic, it was standing proof that things can really get better: *Although a swarm of locusts is frightening, it is the concept of hope that shines in this piece. In origami, paper is folded into definite forms, but these shapes can be unfolded again. Although the creases remain, the paper can be folded to something else again.*[94]

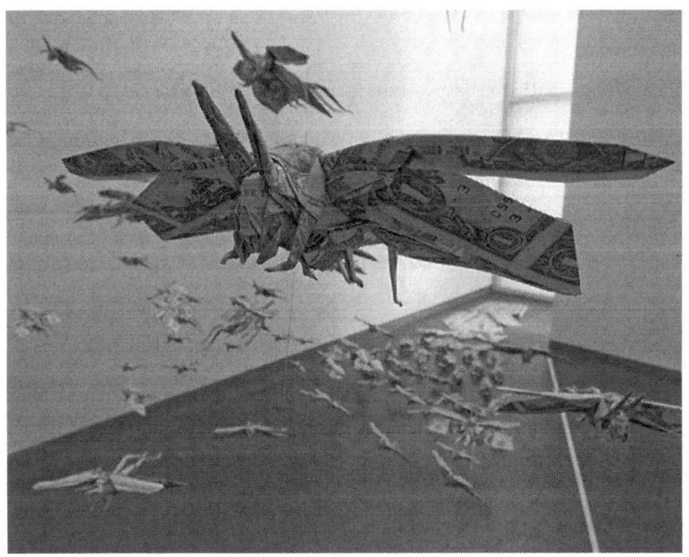

Sipho Mabona, *The Plague* (2012).

Mabona created many more origami sculptures, that range from small to big animals to abstract sculptures to functional lamps. [95]

Moneygami: world leaders in funny hats, *Yosuke Hasegawa*

Japanese graphic designer and origami expert *Yosuke Hasegawa* combined his talents to turn notes from various currencies into depictions of the world leaders and important historical figures wearing various different hats. In an exhibition in Bangkok in 2015, called ***Moneylicious*** one of them was *Abraham Lincoln* in a baseball cap, made of a five dollar bill. He has even created a free Moneygami app that teaches people how to make this Abraham Lincoln Moneygami.[96]

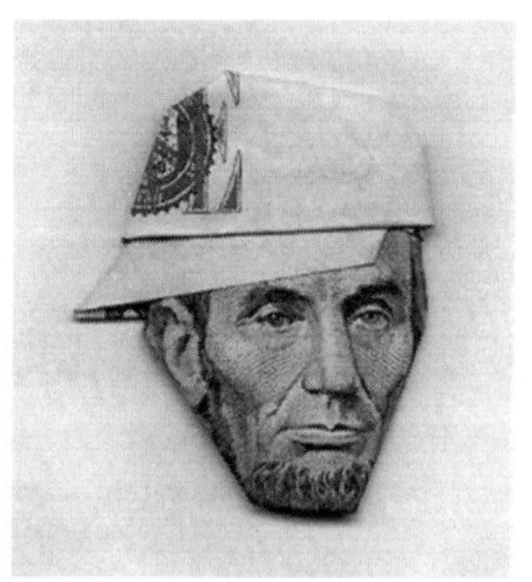

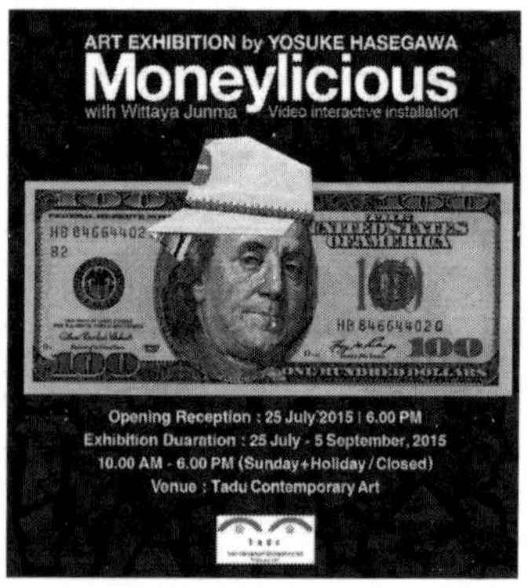

Yosuke Hasegawa, *Abraham Lincoln with baseball cap.*

"Moneylicious" art exhibition 2015. Bangkok, TADU Contemporary Art

(Image courtesy of the artist)

Yosuke Hasegawa made several other Moneygami portraits of Lincoln with different hats and caps, and as said a whole range of other famous figures, like queen Elizabeth in a turban, Gandhi in an Indian 20 rupee baseball cap or Mao Zedong in a cowboy hat from China's one-Yuan slip of tender, gazing at the horizon.

Hasegawa has been bending the currency of various realms since 2006.[97] He has written two books (in Japanese) on the craft. What is his motive to make these Moneygami portraits? *I want to question whether money is the top priority in life or not,* he said.[98] He considers paper money as a representation of an *illusion of peace, created by materialistic businesspeople,'* and asks himself: *'But what's the real meaning of life?*

In the moneylicious exhibition the Thai multimedia artist *Witaya Junma* gave the show an extra interactive dimension with three video installations interpreting Hasegawa's work. In one of them, **Money Face**, the image of the visitor appeared standing half-body-length on a vertical television screen, with a random array of Hasegawa's folded banknote faces superimposed on his head. *Banknotes only bear portraits of important figures,* Junma said, *but I wanted to insert pictures of ordinary people.*[99]

When Hasegawa just started making Moneygami, he gave a work to his niece on New Year's day, and she said: "You can't play with money." Which is exactly what he is doing and now he is making a living out of it.

Moneygami: dollar animals, vehicles and mythical creatures, *Won Park*

Won Park (1979) is an origami master based in Hawaii, dubbed the 'money folder'. When he was faced with the choice of *making money or making art*, Park chose both. His canvas is the United States Dollar Bill. When he was five years old, his mother took him to a Japanese Paper shop, where he bought his first origami folding books. In high school he started developing origami models from dollar bills. With no cutting, tearing or pasting, Park is able to incorporate the details on the bills into his model designs. His own favorite model is the **koi carp**, a one dollar koi folded in such a way that the patterns on the dollar bill become the scales on the fish, and even the facial features fall in exactly the right place.

Generally Won Park works with the United States One Dollar Bill, but he has been branching out to other currencies as well, to add color and vibrancy to each object he folds. He is also the author of some books on the art of Moneygami:

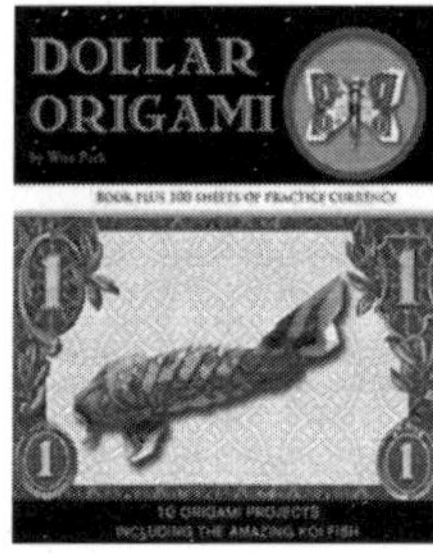

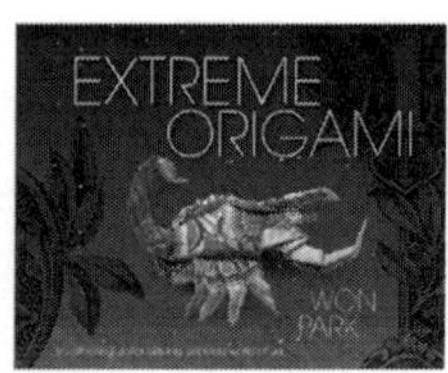

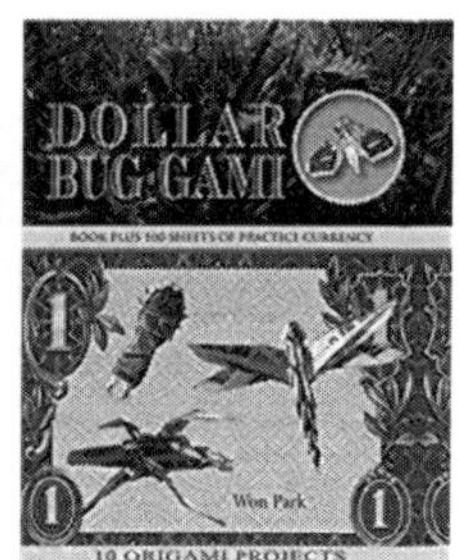

His books all have different Moneygami titles: besides **Dollar Origami** he wrote books on how to fold origami animals and insects, called **Dollar Animal Origami** and **Dollar Bug-Gami**, and one on how to fold war material like a tank, a submarine or a fighter jet, called **Dollar Battle-Gami.** In all these books you find instructions with sheets of practice on how to fold your own origami.

Moneygami with a twist, *Dan Tague*

Dan Tague (1974, New Orleans) found solace in manipulating capitalism in the palm of his hands.[100] In 2005 he watched his life wash away before his eyes. When Hurricane Katrina hit, Tague was living in Mid City (New Orleans), which received about 7.5 feet of water, mud, filth, gas, sludge, waste and death. What did the US government do to help? Hardly anything. Tague felt overwhelmed by abandonment. The shortcomings of the US government and its failure to protect the victims of the Hurricane by building a proper levee fueled Tague's desire to communicate messages about capitalism and its hypocrisies in his artwork.[101]

He began to create messages about the United States government on the very tender issued by the Treasury. He does so by creating intricate layers of folds on currency. His work is not really origami because the dollar bills he uses are not new and these recycled bills aren't perfectly folded. They look more crumpled, like they just came out of a trouser pocket. Tague has said that his art was *as if someone is talking to me through my folded money.*[102]

Tague started doing this kind of art by chance. He was sitting on a bus and playing with a dollar bill.[103] He already liked playing with words and twisting their meaning, and so the two actions came together and a new art form was born. He uses all denominations of US currency, but the majority of the messages comes from the one dollar bill, followed by a five and twenty. The search for the dollar messages usually begins with the bills from his own wallet or crumpled in his pocket. He searches the bill to determine if a message is possible. Folded anywhere from 30 to 200 times without destroying the bill and without cuts or glue, the folds carry a loaded message in a neatly packaged composition.[104] Examples of his messages are: END IS NEAR, TRUST NO ONE, HOLY SHIT, and WE NEED A REVOLUTION.

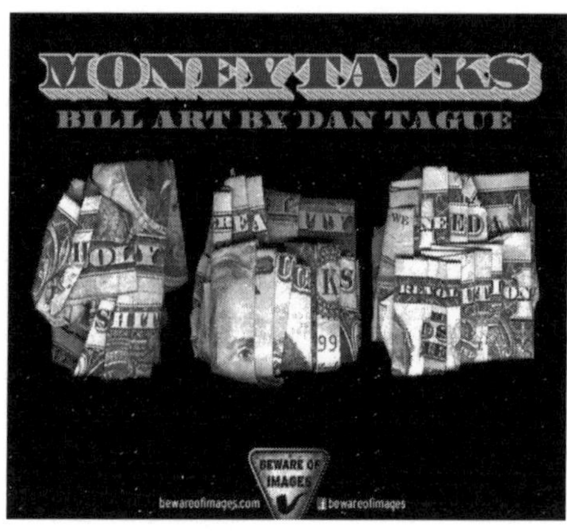

A pyramid of shredded dollars: Evergreen,
Jason Hughes

The work of Jason Hughes (1978, Jacksonville, Florida) is rooted in the abstract relationship between labor, value, and wealth, focusing on the deconstruction and repurposing of physical currency.[105] His process and product address issues of high and low craft, production and trade, as well as shifts in representation and the perception of value. For the last several years he has focused his work on the history of American economic power and its influence over cultural representation in the United States. His artistic work is quite diverse including textiles, collages, and cast sculptures from shredded currency.

A famous example of the last category is his ***Evergreen*** from 2015, a decaying pyramid built with blocks made from shredded cash. The *Federal Reserve* gave him 1,000 pounds of shredded, decommissioned currency, about $2.5 million. From this amount he bundled approximately $1.5 million that looked like a giant pile of grass clippings. The rest of the shredded money he used for other pieces of money art, like ***Another Day Another Dollar***, where the *shredded dollars are woven together into a distinctly monetary rug design.*[106]

On the meaning of *Evergreen* Hughes said: *It's really about how unfettered capitalism and money in politics are eroding our democracy. A pyramid is not just architectural, it's representative of hierarchy, and in* **Evergreen** *the hier-*

archy is crumbling.[107] Hughes discovered that *working on **Evergreen** was actually really fun.* He started washing the money to prep the material for casting bricks, and by the end of the day what was left was *this oily, brown, smelly water (...), the residue from our daily transactions, something that connects all of us as it passes through our hands.* The money that flows between us, connecting every laborer, consumer, and billionaire throughout the world, makes all of our hands dirty. What did Hughes do with *this oily, brown, smelly water*? He boiled this residue down until it was a thick, muddy sludge that he used as a watercolor pigment! He started sketching landscapes with it that are threatened by neoliberal policies and climate change due to those policies. In this way too he gave some critical artistic comments on the inevitable contradictions between the environment and the economy.

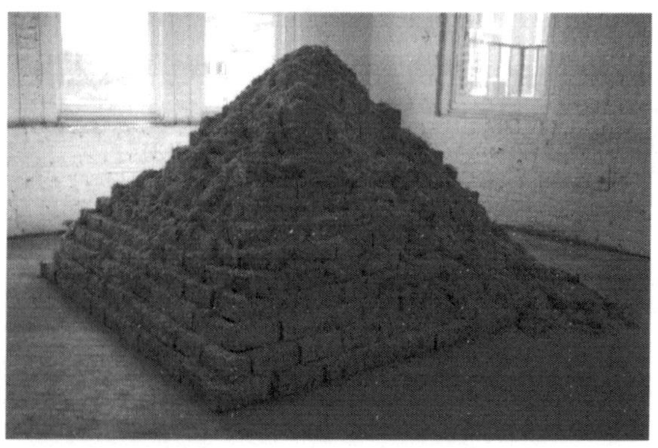

Jason Hughes, *Evergreen* (2015); 192 x 244 x 244 cm.

(Image courtesy of the artist)

Moneyball: Power Spheres, *Alberto Echegaray Guevara* alias *Cayman*

In 1991, *Alberto Echegaray Guevara* (1970, Caracas) was an advisor to the Argentinean economic minister who pegged the Argentine peso at a 1 : 1 rate with the US dollar. He was also a successful entrepreneur, a political scientist, and a regular commentator on CNN. Some say this 1 : 1 pegging of the peso to the dollar contributed to the 2001 economic crisis, leading to a big devaluation of the Argentine peso: the peso-dollar exchange rate dropped to 12 : 1 in 2014. This led to the artistic debut of the former economic advisor under the pseudonym *Cayman* who took on inflation as its subject. His work **Moneyball: Power Spheres** shows the exchange rate 12 : 1 in twelve Murano crystal orbs. Eleven of them are stuffed with one million shredded, out-of-circulation Argentine pesos. A 12th globe is labeled "U.S. Fed" and holds USD $1 million. Seen together they offer a provocative, but already outdated illustration of the peso-dollar exchange rate of that time.

Echegaray got the idea for the project when he visited the US Treasury Department's printing and engraving division and saw the translucent tubes that suck up the cash to be destroyed.[108] *Guevara was struck by the vision of millions of dollars sitting in glass tubes, waiting to be shredded and thrown out,* Sarah Page Maxwell wrote in 2014.[109] *These millions of dollars had passed through possibly millions of hands, and were used to pursue dreams, buy houses, and support families. But with a quick trip through a shredding machine, they were to be rendered valueless.* The central theme in *Moneyball* is this concept of destruction. The artist wanted to break something down to give it a new meaning, or to see what new meaning it would be given. Friedrich Nietzsche once said: *If a temple is to be erected, a temple must be destroyed.*[110] *Moneyball* was Caymen's attempt to give money a new value by destroying its conventional meaning. It was his first work of art and kind of *a mission to discover the hidden symbolism and history behind modern society's relationship with money,* Sarah Page Maxwell wrote.[111] Guevara asserted that the symbolism of the $ sign is also related to the association between slavery and money, and that's no coincidence, he said, because this $ sign was originally used to brand on the faces of slaves.

The first question of anyone who saw the crystal spheres was invariably: *Whose money is this?* or *Where/how did you get the money?* All of the bills were out of circulation, already rendered valueless in the traditional sense (shredded). Echegaray asked permission to take the shredded money in the US Fed and at the European Central Bank. [112] He eventually acquired two bags filled with $2 million worth of old notes from the Federal Reserve. The Argentine Central Bank was the only institution withholding it, though. An ironic move, according to the artist, given that the Argentine peso was the least valued of all the currencies in that time.[113] But he was not surprised, *considering how secretive the country is when it comes to its books, having reported inflation rates for years now as much lower than what independent economics asses.*[114] So how did he acquire the pesos then? Well, for months he followed trucks with out-of-circulation bills to wade through dumpsters with their discards until he finally accumulated enough for the installation.[115]

The artistic practice of Cayman is tied to the hidden influence of the global monetary systems, and the effect of consumerism on spiritual values. His artwork also reflects his fascination with ancient symbols and sacred geometry. That's why he used twelve spheres for *Moneyball*: *A perfect sphere is a symbol of totality, uniformity, concurrency, and original perfection,* he said. *It is eternal, and has no beginning and no end.(...) the circular shape of the sphere represents the eternal "now" in which we exist, and a concept of perfection that we chase through the accumulation of monetary wealth.*

With Moneyball I conclude this chapter on artists who were inspired by the worlds' number one currency, the US dollar, which has the privilege to be accepted all over the world, and is on top of the currency pyramid: key currency, master currency, and dream currency.[116]

4

Art = Money

Art as a currency

At times, many commodities have been used as currencies in certain circumstances. Anything from cattle, corn, beads, shelves, rice, salt, and a lot more including the precious metals gold and silver, whether or not being coined. Even slaves have been used as means of exchange.[117] Can art be considered as a currency too?

In the preface of this book I quoted *Damien Hirst*, who once said that art is the most important currency, and *Joseph Beuys* who wrote **Kunst = Kapital** on blackboards and banknotes. Beuys is supposed to have been the first artist who repeatedly posed this equalization, by which he made clear that to him art has a monetary foundation of value in itself.

But there is a problem with considering art as money, and that's the question of fungibility. The main difference from the dollars and yuans we keep in banks is that art objects are singular. Every art object is different, there are no two works of art with the same value. However, although art differs from money because of the lack of it's fungibility, there is also a similarity, and that is art's lack of intrinsic value or usefulness, which compellingly aligns it with money itself.[118]

Yet organized crime steals artworks not to appreciate its aesthetic value but to use it as a cash substitute in underworld transactions. *Alan Lacoursière*, a former detective with the Montreal police who specialized in recovering stolen artwork, said that in most cases *The artwork remains a form of cash throughout. They remain hidden away in a closet. It's not like in the movies, where some guy who really appreciates art has a secret room in his mansion (where he displays it). I have never seen that in my entire career.*[119] He added he has seen cases where expensive paintings ended up in Russia or Colombia and were used to purchase drugs from drug traffickers based in those countries.

When you look at art as a currency, a distinction can be made in the kind of currency you are referring to: a **social currency** or a **physical currency**. Many art buyers are motivated by aesthetic, intellectual and cultural reasons, but others are buying access to an emerging social class of global capital. Art Advisor *Barbara Guggenheim* backed up that point in the New York Observer:[120] *At a recent dinner, a Frenchman of my acquaintance told a German he'd never met:* ***"You have a Mike Kelley, I have a Mike Kelley."*** *This meant:* ***"You have a million dollars to piss away, I have a million dollars to piss away. You got to the head of the line. I got to the head of the line. We can be friends."*** *It's a secret handshake. If all it takes to get a membership in this elite club is several million dollars, for people who have tens or hundreds of millions, it's cheap at twice the price. And the* *more exoteric works they buy, the better. Hanging and preserving an expensive peace no one understands provides not only the aura of wealth but also the impression that the owner is one of the rare intellectuals who really "gets it".* Here art is used as a social currency and also as a physical currency that one must purchase and spend (think donating it to a museum) to realize its value. Because art is a widely used currency in this way, Citibank is providing a legitimate service to its clients when it advises them on the value of that currency.[121] In that sense, commenting on paintings is no different to giving guidance on the Swiss Franc.

Trompe l'oeil Money

So far I discussed art in general as a kind of currency. Now I turn to artists who present their art more directly as a sort of money. Remember Marcel Duchamp who paid his dentist in 1919 with the check he designed himself: the **Tzanck Check** I mentioned in the preface. Probably the most famous money artist who drew and spent his own money was JSG Boggs. But before I have a closer look at him, I will visit some artists who belong to the category of *trompe l'oeil* painters. As said in chapter two, trompe l'oeil painting is a "fool the eye" technique, in this case still life paintings of bills and coins in such detail that viewers were tempted to pluck them of the canvas.

As a painting style, trompe l'oeil has a history extending back as far as 400 BC. It was part of the culture of Greek and Roman Empires, where horses are said to have neighed at a mural of horses they recognized.[122] The only ancient trompe l'oeil murals that survive today are those unearthed at Pompeii in Italy. The art historian *Vasari* reports on a story of contest in ancient times, held between two renowned painters to see who was the finest. The first painter made a still life so convincing that birds flew down to peck at the painted grapes. The master then turned to his opponent in triumph and said: "Draw back the curtains and reveal your painting." At that moment the second painter knew he had won, because the "curtains" were part of the painting.

Some famous 19th century trompe l'oeil artists in the money painting genre are *Victor Dubreuil, William Michael Harnett, John Haberle, John Frederick Peto, Charles Alfred Meurer,* and *Otis Kaye. The biographies of the money painters often reveal some traumatic event in their lives that brought about their obsession with the fictions and faiths that underlie the value of money. Artists who lost all in crash,* Douglas C. McGill wrote in his article *Money is the Subject, Art the Object.*[123] In 1988 an exhibition of the 'money painters' was held at the *Berry-Hill Galleries*, on the Upper East Side of Manhattan, and that was no coincidence, according to the art historian Bruce Chambers, who organized the exhibition: *The new interest in money painters (...) has come about because many economic and social concerns of America in the late 19th century are similar to those of today.*[124]

What made money such a popular subject for these trompe l'oeil artists? Many of them painted in the last decades of the nineteenth century, a time of materialism and financial empires – the Gilded Age. *It was the era of the Greenback party, with its promise to issue great quantities of treasury notes if elected (causing the public anxiety over the stability of the currency). These artists were also playing with the notion of value, by asking viewers to consider the value of, for example, a real five dollar bill versus the value of a five dollar bill rendered as a work of art.*[125]

Barrels full of painted bank notes, *Victor Dubreuil*

In chapter two we met *Victor Dubreuil*, where I discussed his **The Cross of Gold**, a classic of the money-painting genre. Dubreuil is the same artist who rendered barrels stuffed with bills. This late 19th century master of the trompe l'oeil genre is enigmatic and his life was a bit of a mystery. In Paris he worked as a bank clerk, and stole 500,000 francs from his bank (though he termed it borrowing) and left the bank bankrupt.[126] He was deeply interested in social politics, and some say he stole the money as a political gesture.[127]

When he arrived in New York on June 6, 1882, he found work again in a bank. But soon he was painting still life pictures while teaching himself how to paint. *He used trompe l'oeil illusionistic painting techniques to depict objects, placing them in context with one another to convoy complex allegories that related to social elements of the time and tied to his interest in leftist politics*, Steve Roach wrote in *Coin World*.[128] Dubreuil painted money in practically every form he could imagine: loose bills stuffed into overflowing barrels (remarkable: one of his barrels filled with money is called *Money to Burn*, an oil on canvas from 1893. In chapter one you read about money burning – but there it was about real money burning, here it's metaphorically meant), wrapped bills arranged compactly inside a safe, or a few notes tacked up on a dark wall in an X-shape. Sometimes he painted a single note all by itself in the manner of a portrait.[129] He also painted a picture of bank robbers taking money out of a till, called *Don't Make a Move*. *Here a man with one eye closed points the barrel of a revolver at the viewer. A woman bank robber grabs trompe l'oeil paper money bills from the money drawer. You, the viewer, are absorbed into the painting as the teller in his pawn shop or money changer's stall,* Marc Shell writes.[130] The eye, or *oeil* of the looter, *is the trompe l'oeil of the piece, figuring both the eye of the robber (...) and also the I of the artist who draws his material from the visual realm. It is the same eye that stares (...) from the pyramid in many American dollar bills*.[131] According to Jonathan Clancy, the robber on the painting features the only depiction of the artist.[132]

During his life, Dubreuil's work once was shown in the *Seventh Street Saloon* in New York. His paintings were placed around the saloon, in the words of one contemporary writer *to impress visiting "guys" with ideas of untold wealth.*[133] Some visitors thought his money was a kind of scam, involving counterfeit money. *The New York Herald* wrote that the paintings lining the saloon's walls were *done by an old man who represented a million dollars on canvas three feet square for a fee of twenty dollars or so.*[134] Dubreuil was upset by this characterization, replying in a letter to the editor: *I painted the pictures referred to but was paid a great deal more than the sum mentioned and never believed, nor do I now believe, the pictures were intended to further any evil purposes. As I am well known on the west side as the painter of these pictures I trust, out of justice to me, you will print the above.*[135]

Is it real? *John Haberle, William Michael Harnett, Charles Alfred Meurer*

John Haberle (1856-1933) was born in New Haven, Connecticut, to Swiss immigrant parents. At the age of fourteen he left school to apprentice for a bookplate designer and engraver. There he learned the precision of hand-and-eye coordination necessary for detailed representation.[136] He was also painting display cases and doing odd jobs at *Yale University's Peabody Museum of National History.*

In 1884 he entered the National Academy of Design in New York, where he saw trompe l'oeil painting for the first time.[137] In 1887 he painted *Imitation*, which was exhibited at the National Academy (now in the collection of the *National Gallery of Art* in Washington). It is a painting of various coins and paper money including a Large Size note and a piece of Fractional Currency.

In painting this work, Haberle took a risk. The year before, in 1886, a colleague of him, *William Michael Harnett*, was arrested for counterfeiting. After that, Harnett stopped making trompe l'oeil images, but Haberle ignored warnings by the Secret Service and Treasury Department about his suspiciously accurate paintings of currency due to the fear of counterfeiting and made it his specialty. He continued painting greenbacks throughout his years of greatest productivity. *The Changes of Time* (1888) is one of them, and became a sort of icon of the currency school of painting.

Haberle exhibited work at art institutions, but due to the popular appeal of his style and subject matter, his work was also shown in venues not conventionally known for displaying art, such as bookstores, saloons, liquor stores, and hotels.[138] After his death in 1933 his paintings were virtually unknown until 1948, when art historian Alfred Frankenstein discovered thirty of his works.[139] Frankenstein proclaimed Haberle the *greatest American master of the (trompe l'oeil) tradition*.[140]

William Michael Harnett (1848-1892) was an Irish-American trompe l'oeil painter known for his still-life of ordinary objects. He is credited with founding the trompe l'oeil style in America.[141]

Born in Clonakilty, County Cork, Ireland during the time of the potato famine, his family emigrated shortly after his birth to America. As a young man he made a living by engraving designs on table silver, while also taking night classes at the Pennsylvania Academy of the Fine Arts. Later, in New York he studied at Cooper Union and at the National Academy of Design.[142] Harnett painted things like musical instruments, hanging game, fire arms, a rusted horseshoe nailed to a board, and a casual jumble of second-hand books set on top of a crate.

Money-painting was only part of his extensive work. Other artists had included currency in their paintings, but Harnett was the first to focus solely on paper bills and coins.[143] He made them look so real that in 1886 he was arrested for counterfeiting.

A well known example of his money paintings is *Still-Life Five Dollar Bill* from 1877. *New York law officers seized this bill from the saloon where it hung and demanded that Harnett hand over other "counterfeit" paintings. After viewing the painting, the judge advised that "the development and exercise of a talent so capable of mischief should not be encouraged."*[144] As mentioned above, after that incident Harnett never painted money again.

The painting is now in the collection of the *Philadelphia Museum of Art*.

Charles Alfred Meurer (1865-1955) was converted to trompe l'oeil painting when he saw the work of Michael Harnett at the Cincinnati Industrial Exposition of 1886.[145] Born in Germany to American parents, Meurer was raised in Clarksville, Tennessee. He studied with Frank Duveneck at the Art Academy of Cincinnati in the mid-1880s, and pursued additional training at the Academie Julian and the Academie des Beaux-Arts in Paris. *In terms of facture, his paintings bear some mark of his tight academic training in Paris, although in terms of subject matter, his work is much more Germanic in flavor*, according to the *Internet Antique Gazette*.[146]

As a young artist, Meurer received a pivotal commission from Adolph Ochs, editor of the Chattanooga Times newspaper, to paint a still life incorporating the front page of the paper along with books and objects of editorial wisdom, relating to the newspaper industry. Meurer used this theme in many subsequent paintings. Because of this it is said he invented the "editorial sanctum", a genre of still life in which the objects, notably the front of a newspaper, celebrate a particular individual.[147]

In many of his still lifes he included paper currency. A beautiful example of this is *Still Life with Money, Pipe and Letters* from 1914 (Oil on canvas, 11 x 14 inches). *The composition is a deceptively simple on depicting paper and coin currency casually piled on the edge of a table along with books, stamped envelopes and burnt matches and a glazed pipe. Meurer's intent to "fool the eye" is accomplished with precisely rendered surfaces, along with objects that seem to extend beyond the frame and into the viewer's space. The pile of paper money that appears in danger of sliding off the table and on the floor tempts the viewer to reach in and tidy up, all the greater reminder of the artist's skill.*[148]

Like Harnett and the other trompe l'oeil money painters, Meurer's realistic reproduction of money, considered unlawful, frequently landed him in trouble with government officials.

Up and down, *Otis Kaye*

In the 1929 crash *Otis Kaye* (1885-1974) lost his family's $ 150,000 nest egg. Born in Dresden, Germany, Kaye came to Neemah, Michigan with his parents when he was three years old. In 1904 he moved to New York for a short time. There he discovered his passion for art. With his mother he moved back to Germany where he studied engineering and draftsmanship. He returned to the United States around 1914 and worked as an engineer in Illinois until the Stock Market Crash of 1929.

Sometime in the 1920s he began to paint, focusing on the subject that would continue to be his main inspiration through virtually all of his output: money.[149] *At first he emulated the great American trompe l'oeil painters of the 19th century (...), making comparatively simple compositions of paper money and coins.*[150] Because the US enacted a ban on painting currency in 1909, Kaye did not sell his paintings but gave them as gifts to family members and close friends. As his own fortunes changed, he created more complex, layered works *that convey his thoughts on the stock market, luck, morality, corruption and capitalism.*[151]

In 1937 he painted an instructive masterpiece that says it all: **D'-JIA-VU?** The title is a pun on *déjà vu* that refers to Dow Jones Industrial Average. In this work Kaye painted bonds and currency bills in the trajectory of the stock market, from the 1929 crash (when he lost his family's reserve) to 1937, when the economy was heading into another recession. Below are cards, dice and chips, labeled "Wall St. Poker Co.": a clear indication that links investing with gambling. *Tobacco packs carry the telling names "Old Gold", "Bond Street" and "Lucky Strike", suggesting that investments may well go up in smoke. A label on the "Bond Street" container reads "A Game of Probab" before reaching a tear, while the "Lucky Strike" pack says "It's toasted". The cards – an ace, king and jack – rest in a case that says "I O U U O ME"*[152] The last letter combination of course should be read as "I Owe You, You Owe Me", making it perfectly clear how Kaye was entangled in the crash.

D'-JIA-VU? can be classified as a calligram, which is an arrangement of the elements to make a literal image of the theme. Kaye made many more calligrams on the money theme, like "Face It, Money Talks" that resembles a smiley face, and "Easy Come, Easy Go" that *takes the shape of a butterfly, with bills fanning in and out of a wallet to form the large wings while a net full of coin rolls and a change purse hang below as the smaller wings.*[153] But **D'-JIA-VU?** is a centerpiece of Kaye's work and was his breakthrough painting.

As said, Kaye never exhibited or sold his painting during his lifetime. Just before his death in 1974 he returned to Germany, but beginning in the 1980s his works were sold at galleries and auctions in New York and quickly moved into public and private collections. In 2002 his prints were exhibited at the Federal Reserve Bank in Washington, DC. In 1996 **D'-JIA-VU?** was sold at Sotheby's for $442,500, then and now the record for a work of Kaye.[154]

Otis Kaye made his trompe l'oeil money paintings some decades after the aforementioned money painters and was never in prison for it. *What was once considered a potentially dangerous form of art by the Secret Service and Treasury Department is now treasured among mainstream art collectors and museums alike,* Sarah Miller wrote in her blog in 2015.[155] *In fact, many numismatics over the years have collected such trompe l'oeil works along with their core coin and currency holdings due to the lovely fusion of art and images of wealth that these works display. Works of this genre can be seen at the Metropolitan Museum in New York*

City, National Gallery of Art in Washington DC, and many more museums as well. Dubreuil, Harnett, and other trompe l'oeil painters reveal to us of the place where artist's imagination connects to and elevates the everyday to something truly special, even transforming the crumpled bills in our pockets into art.[156]

But are they really out of legal trouble from now on, the artists who paint money? Not so long ago, in the 1980's the contemporary money artist JSG Boggs found himself regularly confronted with the law.

***Pursued by the law**, J.S.G. Boggs*

During his life (1955-2017) American money artist 'Boggs', as he preferred to be called, more than once ran into trouble with the authorities. His drawn banknotes looked like counterfeiting to them. He was arrested and put on trial in the US, Australia, and Great Britain. At the *Old Baily* he was charged for "reproducing" the currency, but he argued back that it was the "real" notes that were reproductions – his drawings were originals, never meant to be the real thing. He was acquitted, as he was when he faced the same charges in Australia.

How did he make his banknotes? In his book *Boggs, A Comedy of Values,* Lawrence Weschler accompanies the artist on his tours and describes Boggs's method of working.[157] When on tour, he usually carries a satchel with him, in which his tools are located: a pad with green and black Koh-I-Noor precision pens – *point thirteen millimeters. Thing's so delicate it can stand a few hours of Boggs treatment. In fact, I've got to get another one today. I go through dozens of these, both green and black, at nine dollars apiece. And the paper costs three dollars a large sheet, and what with all the mistakes and rejects, I end up extracting maybe two or three finished drawings per sheet. It costs me a goddamn fortune to draw these bills.*[158] But his bills were never to be mistaken for real: in the final touches on his drawings, he always wrote something deviant from the original banknote, like a miniscule B43I or R72 or LSD in place of the serial number. On the other side of the bills for instance he wrote "This note is legal tender for artists" and instead of "Federal Reserve Note" at the top of the bills he'd written "Federal Reserve Not". But after drawing a bill, Boggs's money artwork is not finished yet. The purpose is to spend it and exhibit the documentation of a complete transaction. For instance: one piece, entitled *The Shirts off My Back*, consisted of his drawing of a one-hundred-Swiss-franc note, the four shirts he was able to purchase with it, and the receipts and change from the transaction.[159]

But although in England and Australia Boggs was acquitted from criminal charges, in America they hardly knew how to deal with him. *In 1992 he had a madcap idea to flood Pittsburgh with one million dollars in Boggs Bills, and see if they could get through five transactions (handlers would* *put thumbprints on the back). The Secret Service warned the city and raided his studio, seizing more than 1,000 pieces of work. They never returned them. (...) Mr. Boggs's career was blighted by fruitless appeals to try and get them back. His legal costs mounted. At his Old Bailey trial he had paid his lawyer with drawings for his services. He now started on a series of $1,000 Boggs Bills sporting a portrait of him by Thomas Hipschen, America's chief engraver of banknotes (itself happily exchanged for a Boggs Bill), to cover a hearing in the Supreme Court, if he could get one. But he was also venturing closer to the edge, toting guns and using methamphetamines, and died before he had got that far.*[160]

As said above, Boggs artwork wasn't finished with the drawing of his banknotes. His aim was to spend them and document the whole transaction (as in *The Shirts off My Back*). He produced banknotes that visually refer to specific currencies: American dollars, British pounds, Deutsche Marks, Swiss francs a/o. His intention was to pay with these bills in the respective country afterwards. As he succeeded in these exchange transactions in several countries, you could say in this way he was involved in the global exchange of art and money. In the next chapter I will have a closer look at money artists, who explicitly engage(d) themselves with that side of money art: global exchange.

5

Global exchange

Around the world with currency

In 1848 John Stuart Mill wrote that the existence of *a multiplicity of national monies* is a barbarism: *So much of barbarism, however, still remains in the transactions of most civilized nations, that almost all independent countries choose to assert their nationality by having, to their own inconvenience and that of their neighbours, a peculiar currency of their own.*[161] I think many money artists will agree with this statement. In chapter 3 for instance we came across the currency collagist C.K. Wilde, who expressed the same view that descended from his childhood, when he traveled to Europe to visit his relatives. Returning in the U.S. he couldn't buy candy with his Deutsche Marks, and he asked himself: *Are we not people of one planet? Why is this money powerful only in one context, useless in another?*

In this chapter I'll visit some money artists who are aware of the problems of the whimsical division of territories, borderlines that can be traced by money and mark the separation between the inside and the outside, entering or leaving.

Sail Away and Dress Sculptures, *Susan Stockwell*

In 2013 Susan Stockwell (1962, Manchester, UK) folded a fleet of ships from global currency that sailed away in the Turbine Hall of the Tate Modern in London. ***Sail Away*** consisted of many small boats made from paper currency, tickets and maps that formed a large-scale flotilla. On her website you can read that she is *a sculptor who makes subtly political work about materials and their inherent content and histories, with injustice and inequality as overarching themes. Her work addresses political, social, ecological and feminist issues, using her trademark motifs and metaphors of maps, stacks, dresses, money, recycled computer components, paper, rubber and other everyday materials and products.*[162]

Sail Away was about the idea of dream carriers, referencing trade and sea faring empires. With these boats she was *thematically navigating the notions of international connectivity, personal and social history, and global exchange.*[163] In mythology boats are symbolic of the transmission from the material to the spiritual world and are carriers of our dreams as well as vessels for adventures, escape and journeys. Coupling these themes, *Stockwell's paper money medium serves to represent the unknown links we have with each other, connecting us to the people who have handled each bill, in far reaching corners of the world.*[164]

Susan Stockwell's immersive ***Sail Away*** *unites these motifs through a single medium: currency.*[165] The banknotes she used were from around the world. She considered them as a *humble, yet ever essential resource (...) a commodity of culture and civilization, with varying countries' conception embedded in antiquity and humanity. Appropriating diverse types of notes (...) Stockwell handcrafted hundreds of small boats, folding, crimping, and sewing the paper payment into a fleet of ships.*[166]

Sail Away is not the only money artwork Susan Stockwell made. She is also well known for instance for a series of ***Dress Sculptures*** from 2010, made from maps and money. A famous example of this series is ***Money Dress***, based on the style of dress worn in the 1890's by British Female Explorers. This specific dress was made *in honour of Catherine Routledge, who fell in a crevice in Panama and was saved by the crinoline when it caught on a tree branch. The dress was made with used paper currency from all over the world.*[167] *The intention was that the whole dress would be made from currency with female figureheads on but they are prohibitively rare. As well as being made in honour of Catherine Routledge the piece is based on the idea of female territory and power being enabled by economic independence.* [168]

Money/Change/Money*, Timm Ulrichs*

What happens when you go abroad and have to change your own currency for another? You lose money. This exchange rate loss is comparable with the loss in the meaning of words when you are translating. There is an analogy between language and money in translating/exchanging one word/currency for another, because it always involves a certain loss in meaning/value.

The German artist *Timm Ulrichs* (1940, Berlin) made a money artwork of this phenomenon in 1968/1978, called *Geld/Wechsel/Geld (Money/Exchange/Money)*. He started with 100 Deutsche Marks (the German currency before the Euro) and exchanged it twenty times at the DVKB (Deutsche Verkehrs-Kredit-Bank). What was left of his initial 100 Deutsche Marks? Only 6 Marks! The rest was lost in 'translating' or exchanging the national currencies (of Germany-Norway-Sweden-Denmark-England-Holland-Belgium-France-Switzerland-Italy-Spain-Austria-Greece-USA-Canada-Mexico-Brasil-Australia-Japan-GUS-Germany). Where had the money gone? To the bank (DVKB) that earned on every exchange transaction through the difference in buying and selling rate and the transaction charges of about 3% on every deal. Ulrichs documented the whole process step by step, put the receipts in a wooden box and exhibited it.

This constant exchange-loss-business suggests that in the end it could lead to a total loss and vanishing of value and meaning, in other words loss of substance. Some say that both systems – money and language – are in a permanent process of abstraction, and that this abstraction goes together with a loss of substance. But I don't think that abstraction has anything to do with the loss of value in the exchange performance of Timm Ulrichs. Sure a shift in the ownership of value (from the artist to the bank), but that's quite a different story.

Artmoney/Change/Money, *Maria Fisahn*

In 1993 *Maria Fisahn* (1949, Geldern, Germany, working in Hamburg) seated herself behind an elongated table in the gallery *Westwerk Hamburg* and started selling her art money. In front of her on the table was a money-box: the artist as cashier. The performance was called *Wir verkaufen unser Geld* (We sell our money). She repeated this performance in 1998 and changed/sold many notes of her art money in this way for real money: *I change my currencies for DM and dollar, skills and acts. I pay photographers, scriptwriters, friends and strangers, pay out services and assistants,* she said.[169]

Her money bills were printed with pictures of for instance strawberries (Erdbeergeld), mussels, a pig's head (Schweinekohle) and iron bars, that refer to barter trade. The pig money refers to the archetype of money, the history of the development of money from rituals and cattle sacrifices. Her money bills served also as a swan song for a handy instrument of payment: our paper money, that perhaps in the near future will be obsolete, because of the march of virtual money. During the performance a cassette was playing with the voice of an eighty years old woman, praying the litany of the money concepts, the money-rap, the swan song of paper money.

Within two years Maria Fisahn made more than 600 bills with different money motives, like *Liebesgeld* (love money), *Brotgeld* (bread money) or *Strafgeld* (punishment money). The bills were made of various materials like silk, paper and rags. Instead of a watermark or silver thread as certificate of authenticity, she imprinted chickpeas: In the old days pea money sometimes was the money of the poor. The nominal value she printed on her money bills varied from 1 to 10 000, sometimes in DM, but more often in an indefinite denomination.

Creating art money bills this way were not the only money artworks she made. In 1996 for instance she subjected fourteen printed sheets to a money laundering, and in 1998 she made a golden umbrella, printed with money motives. In her *shredder dances* (1998/99) she let shredded money vibrate on sound membranes to create an energetic resonant.

The world's garbage, *Máximo Gonzáles*

Mexico City-based *Máximo Gonzáles* (1971, Entre Rios, Argentina) uses international bills as artistic medium. His work often takes the form of large-scale pieces or installations, like in *Big magma CCCLXX-I* from 2011 (200 x 400 cm, money and glue). In this work he *experimented with the textility or textuality of money, transforming bills into thread or yarn with which he has woven elegant tapestries, works which illuminate money's influence in and reliance on the warp and weft of human activity.*[170] On his website you can see a video of how this money cloth was woven.[171] *The work is made from the notes' borders ($20, $50, $100 etc) that were trimmed during the process of fabrication in the Bank of Mexico and is normally destroyed.*[172] *Máximo salvaged it, stuck it together to produce long threads, and weaved it on a homemade loom, based on traditional Oaxacan looms.*[173] You can see the bar codes on different parts of the weave. Each sheet indicates a nominal value, series, bill numbers and quantity in batch. So there's everything to uniquely identify the bills contained. At a closer look you can see the color bars, used for controlling the quality of the printing, alignment, and other security standards.

But *Magma* is by far not the only money artwork González made. For instance: he punched holes in money and stitched it together, almost to the point of its total dematerialization, and one of those works he called *The world's garbage* (2012). For this work he used out-of-circulation money and pins. According to Max Haiven, this was a way *visually echoing the decaying and decomposing garbage to be found in landfills all around the world. (...) There is something post-apocalyptic and melancholic here, as if we are alien visitors observing the wreckage of capitalist totality (...).*[174]

Besides his visual money artworks González did a money performance in several cities. For the Mexico City Art Fair (MACO) in London in 2006 for instance, he sat as an Exchange Bureau teller in an "Bureau de Change" and exchanged trimmed out of circulation banknotes for local currency. The out of circulation money was composed of old Mexican bills, where the corresponding value was cut out of the bill in text. For example: a 20 peso bill had the word TWENTY cut out of it. González was dressed up in a suit and tie, performing these exchanges to anybody willing to participate, respecting the amount written in the cut out bill and the nominal value of local currency – so, when in Mexico, he exchanged 100 defunct pesos for 100 current pesos; in London he exchanged 100 defunct pesos for 100 pounds, and in Miami he exchanged 100 defunct pesos for 100 US dollars.

***Money for Art**, Lee Mingwei*

The Taiwanese artist *Lee Mingwei* (1964), living in Paris and New York City, creates participatory artworks. In 1994 he did a project called *Money for Art* in a café, and he repeated the action later on in a gallery version (1997-2000). The original project documented the fate of nine small origami forms made from ten-dollar bills that he created for passersby in a café in San Francisco. People were quite interested in what he was doing with the money. When they were, he started a conversation with them for about forty minutes. During this interaction he would talk about whether something could be money and art at the same time, and about the value of the artwork. Then he said to them: *You can have this piece of artwork. However, I need your phone number so that I can call you back every six months.* Nine individuals accepted his offer. *In exchange for one of these small sculptures, nine of these individuals agreed to stay in touch with me for a year. After six months, two of the individuals had transformed their origami into money by unfolding and spending them, and I photographed their purchases. At the end of the year, five of the origami remained folded, one of the origami had been stolen, and three had been exchanged for goods.*[175] One person said she was very hungry, so having a piece of artwork at that time didn't mean anything to her and she used the ten dollars to buy some bananas.[176] Lee Mingwei said that the most interesting person for him was the homeless man John. Although he was a little bit hesitant to involve a homeless person with a project that dealt with money, he accepted him because his professor said he should just accept whoever would like to participate. So, he gave John one piece, and whenever he got back to San Francisco, he visited him and gave him another. And what did John do with the money? Every time he took the origami money out of his wallet and said: *Look, I still have the artwork.* He collected about twelve of them in his wallet, and *he was actually quite happy that someone involved him in a project that deals with money, and he is very proud that he didn't spend any of them.*[177]

What did the others do with their money artworks? Some had kept it, others had bought Haagen-Dazs ice cream, a Paul Simon CD or moccasins, and one sculpture was stolen from a student. *In this work the individual appreciation of art and of the original origami sculpture's monetary value is reflected*, Stefan Haupt writes.[178]

For the gallery version of *Money for Art* Mingwei *invited participants to take an origami one-dollar bill from a compartment in one of three multi-compartment shelves mounted on the walls, and to leave in exchange any object they considered to be of equal value, along with a card on which they wrote their first name and their profession. The objects left in exchange included a bottle of Prozac, a credit card with pin number, and a condom; one visitor left only the card, with her first name and the word 'thief'.*[179]

I think *Money for Art* is a beautiful example of what's happening when one thing transforms into another.

Cultural symbols*, Barton Lidicé Beneš*

The American sculptor *Barton Lidicé Beneš* (1942-2012) worked in materials that he called artifacts of everyday life and one of those artifacts was money. Among other things he made sculptures from chopped up, everyday American cash, purchased pre-shredded from the Federal Reserve. He entered the art scene during the 80's with a shredded United States currency collage art work of the *Virgin Mary*. This work was followed by a series of other money art works, like his *Money Shoe* (1980), created from chopped up American currency and pre-Mao 10 Yuan Chinese notes, decoupaged on an actual platform heel.[180] In 1986 he made a *Reconstruction* of shredded dollars, put back together on a loom, in 1992 he put a dollar egg in a basket of shredded money and called it *Nest Egg*, and in 1993 he created some cooking utensils with Portuguese CEM Escudos, called *Haute Cuisine*.[181] Another mixed-media money artwork is titled *Money Lighthouse* (1996, app. 19.5"W x 27"H),[182] depicting a shining lighthouse above waves, rendered in disassembled global currency on deckle-edge paper.

Since a currency's visual design is always a mirror of a country's culture, history and politics, the artistic exploration of cultures is an important subject of money art. In 2000 Barton Lidicé Beneš made a series of money art works from folded banknotes in forms that represented cultural symbols from the notes' respective countries of origin. The cultural symbol he chose for the American dollar was a pillbox, in which the box as well as the pills coming out of it were folded from dollar bills. For Great Brittan he folded a tea bag from the British pound, France was represented by a snail's shell, Germany by some crown caps made from Deutschmarks, Japan by a Sushi roll of yen, and for India he made a Bed of Nails of a rupee bill. As a final example in this range of Beneš's money artworks I mention his choice for the little bit nasty cultural symbol of *Afghanistan*[183] in the form of a hypodermic needle...

***Give me my fucking money!**, William Powhida*

American artist *William Powhida* (1976, New York City) has become known as something of a gadfly of the art establishment. In 2004 he *began compiling lists of enemies, rendering portraits of each enemy in graphite and gouache with insults written beneath each face.*[184] His father was also on the list, identified by the word "failure" under his portrait.

Powhida uses pencil diagrams to illustrate the way power and money influence the art world. *They are aimed, in part, at puncturing the overinflated myth that the realm of contemporary art is based on the noble and unassailable virtues of aesthetic value alone*, Max Haiven wrote.[185] In 2010 Powhida made a drawing, called *A Guide to the Market Oligopoly System* (graphite on paper, 11x14 inch = 29x36 cm). *It's dominated by a big pyramid, with the yearning masses at the bottom – submerged artists, deep in debt, with enthusiasm rather than money*, Felix Salmon wrote in his 2010 blog.[186] In this pyramid Powhida explains the economic conditions that most artists find themselves in: *There are always more people who like to earn their income as a artist than there is demand for them: there is a structural excess supply of labor. So, why do they persist?*[187] Well, *it's a labor of love, or willful ignorance of the odds*, Salmon commented.[188]

Another big piece of Powhida is *Griftopia* (2011), a ten-foot-wide visual interpretation of Matt Taibbi's book of the same name.[189] The layout calls to mind a spider's web which *implicates bankers, regulators, broadcasters, libertarian ideologues and successive presidents and secretaries of the Treasury in a concerted effort to install free market doctrine in Washington and beyond*, Paul Crosthwaite writes.[190] *At the centre resides Alan Greenspan, the former Chairman of the Federal Reserve whose celebrated maintenance of the 'Great Moderation' turned out merely to be preparing the way for the Great Recession.*[191] In the center of *Griftopia* Alan Greenspan is depicted as "The Biggest Asshole Of The Universe".

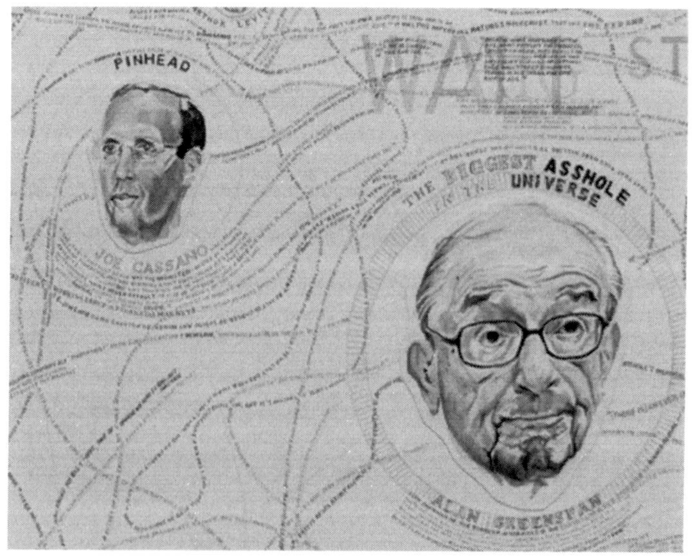

William Powhida, Detail of *Griftopia* with Alan Greenspan in the centre of the web.

***The Artist as a Currency Converter**, Dadara*

When the Dutch artist *Dadara* (Daniël Piotr Rozenberg, 1969, Łódź) launched his *Exchanghibition Bank* at the beginning of 2011, he announced that he started his *own bank as an artist, because governments had no money for Art, but lots of money to bail out banks*, as he told Anna Batista in an interview.[192] It puzzled him *that art seemed to be mostly valued because of its financial worth in our society,* and not for its spiritual, artistic or social value.

Until that time the artist wasn't very interested in money, *because, as so many artists, I come from an anti-money background.*[193] But as a true bank director of the *Exchanghibition Bank* he became *fascinated and even obsessed by money.* Now that he was using money as his artistic material, he needed to study money and became quickly *fascinated by this abstract material, not backed by any tangible asset, existing in a purely virtual way, and created as debt with one click of a button by banks.* He found out that money is *just an agreement, a form of energy, which, when it is exchanged, has value.* This value comes into being *whenever we use money, it's not a one-way transaction. We do not just buy something from someone, we give something back as well – money.*

A year before he started his own bank, he was already working at his *Pool of Plenty* project: a pool filled with millions of money bills, bundled in stacks. The bills at the pool were not real money, but pieces of aesthetically pleasing art.[194] The pool was protected by security guards. Visitors who wanted a bill though, could buy or rather exchange one at the bank initiated by Dadara: the *Exchanghibition Bank*. This Bank took form as a travelling exchange booth, and was temporarily stationed at pop-up locations like the Central Station in Amsterdam, the *Museum Boijmans Van Beuningen* in Rotterdam, the *Stedelijk Museum* Amsterdam, the *Geldmuseum* in Utrecht, and it also operated at Occupy and in shopping centers. The bank changed Euros into banknotes designed by Dadara himself, printed in bright colors on holographic foil with values from zero to infinite passing thru one million. During this bank performance the banker himself and his associates were dressed in futuristic banker suits with paint splattered trouser hems and shoes. The purpose of Dadara's bank was to raise questions about the value of art and money and other aspects of our society.

To continue this discussion he started a new Art as Money project in 2012, called the *Transformoney Tree*. This tree had the Exchanghibition banknotes hanging as leaves from its branches, but participants were able to pick the Exchanghibition banknotes from the tree, while decorating its bark by gluing real banknotes to it. In this way the bark got covered with real banknotes during a week at the *Burning Man Festival*.[195] This follow-up to the Exchanghibition Bank again dealt with the value(s) of money and art. In the process of interaction the dollar bills lost their financial value, but added to the value of the artwork. According to

Dadara, the *interaction with the Transformoney Tree could help us with the shift from a fragile mono-money-culture to a diversified world of many alternative currencies, providing tools for exchange of various forms of value as a necessary alternative for our current debt-based-system, which is focusing on infinite economic growth on a finite planet.*[196]

***Money Maps**, Justine Smith*

We met Justine Smith before in chapter 3, where I presented her Weapons and dollar series. But now, to conclude this chapter on money artists connecting currencies around the world, I like to visit her once again to have a closer look at her money maps.

In an interview with Jessie Moniz Hardy in The Royal Gazette of July 2016[197] the artist said that the idea for making maps out of currency literally came to her in a dream. *Of all my work, I am probably most proud of my world maps*, she added. Then the interviewer asked to tell her more about one of her maps: the *Money Map of Bermuda* from 2014. Justine answered that it was *by an amazing coincidence, when it was first commissioned Bermuda had their bank notes redesigned. The whole new series of the Bermudian dollar had just come out. My map was directly inspired by the silver seam that runs through the banknotes. I wanted to show off the banknotes as much as I could because they are so beautiful.*[198] One way to interpret her Bermuda Map is to associate it with the Bermuda Triangle, where things just disappear into thin air: Bermuda as a money trap which subsequently makes money disappear as result of being a tax haven. In the Bermuda Triangle anything that enters may not see the light of day once more. The Money Map of Bermuda lends itself also for the connotation that colorful banknotes are subsequently lost within the world as virtual money evolves and marches against tangible money like paper money.

For Justine Smith the idea for making money maps is *that you can read the maps politically, historically and culturally from the imagery on the bank notes. You can learn so much about a country by looking at its bank notes.*[199] To put it in a different way: by using bank notes the value systems that surround our idea of money are brought to the foreground, because they present a national identity and an insight into a countries politics, history, religion, economy, and culture. During an exhibition of her money maps at *The Map House* in London in 2015, the artists' exploration into the importance and function of civilization through her maps complimented the selection of original maps.

As a final example of Justine's money maps I mention her *Time is Money* from 2011. It is a world map divided into international time zones and incorporates sections of banknotes from every country in the world, where the countries are made up of pieces of their own currency. A section of a banknote from every country of the world is cut into thin strips, amalgamated, and then divided into time zones. This amazingly detailed artwork again shows her fascination for the way banknotes reflect the society they represent through the images of national heritage, wildlife, industry or leaders they chose to celebrate and glorify. *Time is Money* is a departure from the idea that the world is shown by continent only: there are no political boundaries at all.

6

In Art We Trust

A ring of believers

Art, like money, is a commodity with an unfixed, intangible value. The worth of both *is subject to forces that have little to do with the physical properties of a painting on a wall or a bill in a wallet*, Melissa Starker wrote, and I couldn't agree more.[200] The value of art and money *is a convention that depends on collective states of minds like trust and confidence,* noted Tyler Cann, associate curator of contemporary art at the Columbus Museum of Art.[201] So the value we attribute to art and money is simply an act of faith. There is no material, real value involved in money and most art. Art, like money, is a mind thing.[202] That's one of the reasons that the United States decided to adopt the phrase "In God We Trust" as the nation's motto in 1956 and print it on their paper money. The first paper currency bearing the phrase entered circulation on October 1, 1957. However, long before, in 1864, this motto already appeared on the Two-cent coin, but not on paper currency.

In 2014 the artists *Roger Hiorns* and *Paul Ramirez Jonas* invited visitors in the Columbus Museum of Art to remove the religious from U.S. currency by hammering the "God" off their spare change or drop a coin into a penny-punching machine and walk away with a souvenir coin embossed with lettering that can read as either "We Trust" or "Trust Me".[203] But in who or what do we trust when it's no longer our trust in God or Gold that backs up the money? In 2014 Erin Fletcher suggested that *we can trust that change will happen regardless of money or ruling system.*[204]

Do we trust ourselves enough to accept the fact that money is just a piece of paper or credit in the form of a virtual bank account, covered by nothing else but faith? Does this end up to the conclusion that by now we can paraphrase the proposition of *Marshall Mc Luhan* by saying that 'money is the message'?[205] Has money itself become our God who represents our faith? The Money Mammon? Or, to put it differently: is the message (of trust) embedded in the medium?

For an attempt to answer that question I like to go back to the painting of *Quentin Massijs, The Money Changer and His Wife*, with which I started chapter 2. In the sacred book lying in front of the banker's wife we see a picture of the holy Mother who *balances her sacred book arm-in-arm with the Child while the wife, who is conspicuously childless, hardly manages her ocular seesaw between sacred book and money.*[206] In chapter 2 I said that the banker's wife is distracted by the look of the money and imagines she sees a representation of wealth, power, prosperity etc. But now that I am speaking of Trust, we might also deduce from the painting that it represents a shift from faith in God to faith in money. Trust is the keyword for the acceptance and functioning of money, hence the shift from "In God We Trust" to "In Money We Trust" is not a bad thing, but many people's trust doesn't reach that far and they still demand some kind of backing or security for their money. In that case, who or what will back and protect the stability of their money if it's no longer God or Gold? Could it be Art?

For the purpose of functioning as backing for our monetary system today we see an increasing use of art, especially the so called 'Blue chip' art. This 'Blue chip' art, like the blue chip stocks, the term is derived from, provides a relatively safe investment. That's a major reason that bankers and financial specialists are the largest group of buyers on the international art market today, mostly through the auction houses like Sotheby's and Christie's, which represent blue chip artists like Hirst, Murakami and Koons. *In our current cosmopolitan, materialistic, evidence-based world where many of us are suspicious – or even disdainful of – religion,* (blue chip) *art might be an ecumenical, secular religion,* Anna Deavere Smith wrote.[207] In the 21st century art has become an investment vehicle: art as stock. A kind of stock the investors hang on their walls or put on pedestals like holy relics to show and impress their friends and business relations, or store them in vaults as investments. *The reeling prices of artworks in the 1980s – a period of excess capital and demand for no ascetic goods – recall those of the traditional relic-and-icon markets in medieval Christendom*, Marc Shell notes.[208] Art has always been an object of financial as well as spiritual investment. That's why art, especially blue chip art, has two faces: a shallow holy face on one side and a quasi money face on the other side of the coin. That's why this kind of art is collected, stored and shown in temples especially erected for the purpose to admire and gaze at these works: museums like churches to worship the art in which we trust.

As you may remember, Joseph Beuys more than once said and wrote that Art = Capital, and this statement especially applies to the blue chip art. And as these artworks can function as security for credit and also as a cash substitute (particularly loved in underworld transactions as I described in chapter 4), this art is not only capital, but also money, surreal money. The value of this surreal art money stems from a secular religious belief: In Art We Trust. And what do people do when they trust someone or something? When they have faith in a person or a thing? They spend money for him/her or it.

Some money artists used this faith to create artworks. The first one I present to you is *Caleb Larsen.*

Dollar bill acceptor, collected money*, Caleb Larsen*

In 2009 the American conceptual artist Caleb Larsen (1979) exhibited his *$ 10,000 Sculpture (in progress). Dollar bill acceptor, collected money.* It consisted of a standard dollar bill acceptor found in soda and candy vending machines. *This device has become a symbol of self-service retail transactions*, Larsen wrote on his website.[209] It was installed *seamlessly into a plain white wall with no clues to inform the viewer as to the nature of the piece. Nor does it suggest what might happen if they were to insert a dollar bill.* And that's what the visitors were invited to do: insert a 1 or 5 dollar bill in the machine. The direction to **Insert bill Here** is illustrated with a hand holding a dollar bill in the proper position. The insertion itself is an essential part of the artwork, without this participation it is not complete: *The work exists primarily at the moment of contribution by the viewer. It is a continual charity, or more cynically, a form of panhandling. It asks for money, and offers nothing (by way of direct response) in return. The money that it accepts goes into a fund with a goal of $10,000.*[210] What happened when this goal was accomplished and the work had collected the total of $10,000? Well, then the amount was split 50/50 between the artist and the collector. In this way the work was always "in progress". *Like the avaricious Sisyphus, the work is reaching towards a goal, only to be returned to its starting point upon reaching the goal.*[211]

In this artwork a certain relationship between the artist and the participating visitor is established, because as I noticed above, the peace is not complete without the participation of the visitor: *Meaning, the money is to be considered a material of the piece, not capital.*[212] The question is which visitors are inclined to participate in this piece. Well,

I think those who have faith in the artist, the ones who believe in the artwork, who have Trust In Art, and consider their monetary participation a spiritual investment.

Prada juxtaposed with 99 Cent, *Andreas Gursky*

In the 12th century *Bernard of Clairvaux* wrote that *(…) for at the very sight of these costly yet marvelous vanities men are more kindled to offer gifts than to pray. Thus wealth is drawn up by ropes of wealth, thus money bringeth money; for I know not how it is that, wheresoever more abundant wealth is seen, there do men offer more freely.*[213] Bernard of Clairvaux was one of the medieval reformers who complained that the church had become an economic enterprise where *(…) eyes are feasted with relics cased in gold, and their purse strings are loosed. They are shown a most comely image of some saint, whom they think all the more saintly that he is the more gaudily painted.*[214] But art, like the church, is as indicated above supposed to be a matter of spiritual rather than material riches. However, material riches often seem to play first fiddle in church and art.

The German photographer Andreas Gursky (1955) made photo's of this phenomenon in the 1990's, called the *Prada Series,* depicting empty white shop cupboards as well as the same retail displays filled with Prada shoes. The empty ones allude both to the sacred 'white cube' of the gallery and the temples of luxury consumer goods where products like Prada shoes and bags are sold.

In 2002 the *Schirn Kunsthalle* in Frankfurt made an exhibition with the theme *Shopping*, where the *Prada Series* of Gursky were juxtaposed with his *99 Cent* (2001), a huge photograph of an overloaded supermarket, from which just a few small consumer heads poke out. The photograph was taken at a '99 only store', an American discount, single-price retailer on Sunset Boulevard in Los Angeles. It *depicts its interior as a stretched horizontal composition of parallel shelves, intersected by vertical white columns, in which the abundance of "neatly labeled packets are transformed into fields of color, generated by endless arrays of identical products, reflecting of the shiny ceiling" (Wyatt Mason).*[215]

Andy Warhol said in 1985: *Lock up a department store today, open the door after a hundred years and you will have a Museum of Modern Art. And Rem Koolhaas wrote in 2001 in his book on the New York Prada store: "In a world where everything is shopping... And shopping is everything... What is luxury? True luxury is NOT shopping." If so, the museum is the luxury version of the consumer world.*[216]

***Liquid Assets**, Ori Gersht*

What do we trust? What are our alternatives? When it's no longer Gold or God we can trust to cover for our money, we can at least trust that change will happen regardless of money or ruling system. In 2012 that constant change in our value system was presented by Israeli born (1967), London-based artist *Ori Gersht* in a looping video installation, called *Liquid Assets – A Portrait of Euthydemas II, King of Bactrica 180 BCE.* In this *short, high-definition film a rippling gray blob of molten metal that looks rather like mercury rolls into close-up view against a mottled gray field. Slowly it takes the loose shape of a disk.* After several minutes the image of an ancient silver coin appears *with the powerful head of a king adorned by a diadem.*[217] This king is Euthydemos, *founding warrior-ruler of an ancient Greco-Bactrian dynasty.* He *usually had a depiction of the heroic demigod Heracles stamped on the obverse of his drachmas* and that tells us something about *the king's robust idea of his own omnipotence – and of* ***official art's propaganda role in spreading the opinion.***[218] This last remark is of special interest to me, because it highlights my proposition that art can be used as an extra backup for confidence in a ruler or system. And this observation also suggests that already in ancient times people trusted in art as an extra backup for their money and ruling system.

$49,983 paid and pulped for an Art Degree,
Thomas Gokey

How much trust must you have in art to be prepared to pay 50,000 dollars for an education to become a professional, recognized artist? Do you trust yourself as an artist to earn back your money invested in a MA degree by selling your future artworks? Do you have so much trust in art?

Syracuse University Art Professor *Thomas Gokey* earned his Master of Fine Arts degree in 2007, but remained chained to his alma mater by $49,983 of debt. *Soon after he graduated, the grim prospect of indefinite payments inspired its own art piece. He put his debt up for sale in reconstituted squares of shredded money from the Federal Reserve, which he called* ***Total Amount of Money Rendered in Exchange for a Masters of Fine Arts Degree to the School of the Art Institute of Chicago, Pulped into Four Sheets of Paper*** (2011).[219] Gokey acquired the exact amount of cash that his tuition cost in shredded form from the Federal Reserve Bank of Chicago and then pulped this in four large sheets of paper. The artwork was the act of selling these papers for the amount of money it was made out of. For example, 1 sq inch costs $4.22, one sq ft costs $607.70, etc. He had a full legal contract that everyone signed who purchased a part.

The project got good press, but did he succeed in his intention to redeem his student loan by selling these parts? When I asked him about it in September 2017, he answered: *Unfortunately I have only sold about $1,000 of that artwork. I have a new strategy and I'm currently trying to redesign a website around this new strategy. I've been researching Student Loan Asset Backed Securities (or SLABS for short) and as a part of my research I have been cold calling some Wall Street analysts who specialize in SLABS.*[220] *(...) A few have suggested they might like to buy a little of my debt and* *have even given me referrals to other Wall Street investors who collect art. So my new strategy is to try to get a few very wealthy people to buy my debt.* Once the last piece is sold, Gokey will have paid for his Master of Arts education.

The project was about debt, *something everyone can relate to,* Gokey said. *I am interested in the relationship of value and material, especially given the fact that I just spent so much money for a piece of paper (my diploma). This project is also about the coming university bubble.*[221]

Bankrupt Banks, *Superflex*

Banks make use of art to support and consolidate their brand name. To start with they do so with a company logo, often designed by artists. These kind of artworks are clearly meant to strengthen the public's trust in the solidity of the banks. But what happens after banks go bust or are acquired by governments, other banks or private entities? After the financial crisis of 2008 this happened to dozens of banks and the once powerful companies were suddenly rendered powerless. Banks went bust in a puff of smoke and with it their once high estimated symbolic brand logos vanished into thin air. Originally designed to convey strength, authority and confidence, these now defunct symbols became portraits of failed power structures.

The Danish art collective SUPERFLEX (Jakob Fenger, Rasmus Nielsen, Bjørnstjerne Christiansen) started in 2008 to paint the corporate logos of 24 of the world's defunct banks and turned them into a roomful of banners. *Beginning with the acquisition of the British mortgage lender, Alliance and Leicester by Gruppo Santander on July 14, 2008, the series acts as a sort of timeline, charting the collapse and subsequent reconfiguration of major international financial markets. While all of the works are unique, the series will grow as more banking institutions face either failure or reorganization. Bankrupt Banks will continue to illuminate the failures and irregularities of a global financial system,* Superflex wrote on their website.[222] After this first banner, other banners followed: *Merrill Lynch acquired by Bank of America, September 14, 2008* (2012), *BankWest acquired by Commonwealth Bank of Australia, October 9th, 2008* (2012), etcetera. The banners show us *the vigorous attempts at brand positioning the banks got up to, billing themselves as swooping eagles or soaring palms or homey houses on hills. And all those clever symbols can now only represent failure,* Blake Gopnik wrote in the *Daily Beast.*[223] And in 2012 Karen Archey commented in the *Art Agenda*: *Originally created to communicate power, prestige and success, these logos are ironically banded together with a hilariously deflating effect.*[224] And she adds: *A generous take on "Bankrupt Banks" would be that Superflex obliquely comments on the deflating and re-inflating bubble of the art market, itself an economic system.* Yes, an economic system build on trust, Trust in Art you might say.

The installation is meant to be an open-ended work by the artists. That is, as more banks collapse, more flags can be raised.

How to Build Cathedrals, Insertions to Ideological Circuits, a golden Thread and a Money Tree, and reducing the value of money to nothing, *Cildo Meireles*

In 1987 the Brazilian artist *Cildo Meireles* (1948) composed a narrow tower of 800 communion wafers that teeters high above a sea of 600,000 glittering coins. The sky above the coins and wafers is a canopy of 2000 illuminated large animal bones. The installation is called *Mission/Missions (How to Build Cathedrals)* and alludes to religion, commerce and human loss. It was made for an exhibition to commemorate the Jesuit missions to South America between 1610 and 1767, when the Jesuits were themselves suppressed by the papacy. *Missionaries sought to eradicate cannibalism in the indigenous population by offering the consumption of Christ's body in the sacrament of Holy Communion*, Chantal Powel wrote on her Artists blog.[225] *However using one form of culture to replace and eradicate another can be viewed as a form of cannibalism itself.*

Meireles explained that he *wanted to construct something that would be a kind of mathematical equation, very simple and direct, connecting three elements: material power, spiritual power, and a kind of unavoidable, historically repeated consequence of this conjunction, which was tragedy.*

He *wanted a sky of bones, a floor of money, and a column of communion wafers to unite these two elements.*[226] The 'mathematical equation' can be recognized in the square carpet of 600,000 coins laid out on the floor and the matching suspended square canopy made from 2,000 bones, seemingly held up by the thin eight feet high column of communion wafers. According to James Hall *here, as so often in Meireles's work, mathematics is moralized and given a troublingly tangible architecture.*[227]

The pendulous expanse of bones can be understood as a metaphor for the slaughter of the indigenous peoples brought out as a result of colonial enslavement, Tyrus Clutter wrote in his blog.[228] *Yet, a more contemporary reading might connect the bones to the consumers economics of first world beef production. Brazil has been transformed into one if the world's leading cattle producers. That beef is raised in deforested parcels of land that once hosted the Amazon forests. The allusion to death implied by these bones may also signal the larger ecological impact Western traditions and systems have placed on not only the global south, but the entire planet.*

As the title of the work indicates, *Mission/Missions (How to Build Cathedrals)* clearly has a religious connotation. Meireles is interested in the intertwining relationship between Brazil and the religion of the Europeans, which I guess in his opinion was originally mainly Catholicism. In other artworks, in which he uses Brazilian banknotes, he holds the entrenchment of Catholicism with Brazilian culture in mind: old Brazilian banknotes were called *Cruzeiro*, which circulated in different variations from 1942-1986, first replaced by the cruzado in 1986 and, after a brief period of reinstatement from 1990-93, by the *real* in 1994.

Cruzeiro means *cross* and in the 1970s Meireles produced several works that utilized this currency. He conceived two projects that he called *Insertions into Ideological Circuits* and one of them was his *Banknote Project*. For this project he stamped subversive messages onto banknotes before returning them to normal circulation. The messages include slogans as 'Yankees Go Home', 'Straight Elections', and 'Quem Matou Herzog' (Portuguese for 'Who Killed Herzog'), *referring to a journalist who died in police custody after suspicious circumstances. Meireles stamped the banknotes both sides – his message appearing on one side and the work's title and the artist's statement of appearing on the other.*[229] In 1970, when Meireles produced the *Insertions*, Brazil was suffering the most oppressive period of its twenty-one year military dictatorship. The *Insertions* constituted a form of guerilla tactics of political resistance, which *functioned as a kind of mobile graffiti.*[230] Meireles rubber stamped the banknotes and in this way imitated the method of the Brazilian Central Bank to upgrade the old cruzeiro to a new cruzeiro (cruzeiro novo) in 1967 – the old banknotes revalued with a simple hand stamp, dividing their value by one thousand.

Question: how many of his inserted banknotes did the artist sell? What do you think? None! Why not? Well, because his intention was *that people may stamp their own message on banknotes and themselves send out views or commentary into wider circulation. This may be done in any country, with any currency.*[231]

Meireles is always interested in things that are at the same time matter and symbol, like money, mainly tangible money I think, because money on bank accounts is no longer matter. The conundrums of value have continued to fascinate him. *Meireles creates sculptures and installations that tie everyday materials to larger political and philosophical concerns.*[232] The pairing of substances with vastly different monetary values suggests the precariousness of economic relationships. An intriguing example of this is his *Thread* from 1990-95. *Thread is a modular cube, a form of evocative of the geometric rationality of Minimalist art, but it is constructed of a material generally associated with agriculture. A gold wire encircles the mass of hay. At one end of the wire, a single 18-carat gold needle is inserted to the cube, recalling the common expression, "Like finding a needle in a haystack."*[233] The minute needle is embedded in the massive cube (215.9 x 185.5 x 182.9 cm) *and may call to mind the place of the individual within a larger social system*, according to the website of MoMA.[234]

As a final example of Meireles' money art I like to mention his *Money Tree* (1969). A wad of a hundred one-cruzeiro notes, secured with rubber bands, was presented as an artwork on a pedestal. It was put on sale at a price twenty times higher than this amount. In this way the artist questioned the differences between real, symbolic and exchange value. *Money Tree* pointed towards *the problem of the value of the art object and the discrepancy between use-value and exchange-value*, Meireles said.[235] At the time it was made, in inflationary Brazil, money was the cheapest material to work with, he joked.[236] A nice example of the paradox of symbolic value versus the real value of things.

As a last clandestine fling, Meireles became an ironic counterfeiter. *From 1974 to 1978 he ventured onto the terrain of artistic falsification and produced Zero Cruzeiro and Zero centavo, reducing the value of money to nothing. He also replaced the illustrious figures who usually decorate banknotes with two individuals who are theoretically on the fringe of Brazilian society: an inmate of a psychiatric hospital in Trinidad and a Kraô Indian. In Zero Dollar (Zero Dollars, 1978-1984) and Zero cent (Zero Cents, 1978-1984), he delves into the meaning of monetary, by understanding foreign currency as an iconic representation of a country. In these works money becomes a paradigm of the relations between matter and symbol, since it can be both things at once.*[237]

7

Time is money

The real price of everything

Time-based currency is a currency or exchange system in which the unit of account or value is a time-unit, based on working-hours without the use of money. The idea of using time as unit of exchange appeared shortly after the Industrial Revolution. The origins *can be traced both to the American anarchist Josiah Warren, who ran the Cincinnati Time Store from 1827 until 1830, and to the British industrialist and philanthropist Robert Owen.*[238] He founded *The National Equitable Labour Exchange* in 1832 in Birmingham, England, but failed already in 1834. It issued "Labour Notes" denominated in units of 1, 2, 5, 10, 20, 40, and 80 ours.

The first contemporary time bank was started in 1991 by Paul Glover in Ithaca, New York. People who followed his idea, began to exchange time in the form of "Ithaca Hours", which still flourishes. Today all over the world there are time banks, like *Timebank.cc* in The Netherlands, *Time Dollar* in America, and *Fureai Kippy* in Japan.

However, the idea that the quantity of working hours is all-decisive for the determination of the value of a product,

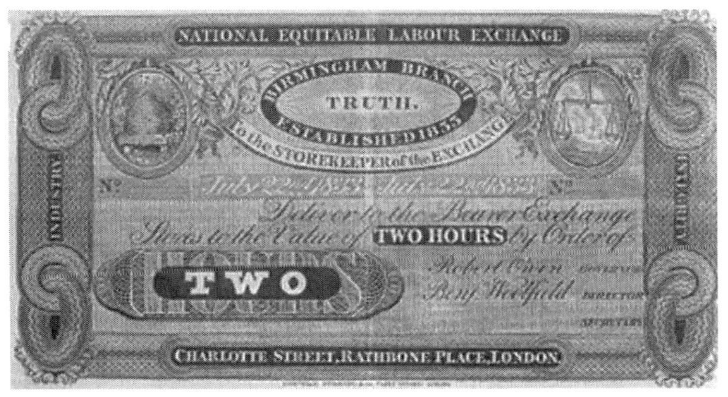

Two hours work Labour Note,

The National Equitable Labour Exchange, 1833

especially the exchange-value, goes back to *Aristotle* in ancient Greek times and *Adam Smith* in 1776 in his famous book *The Wealth of Nations*.[239] In other words, you could say that buying a product is corresponding to buying a quantity of working hours. This idea is elaborated by some money artists in very different ways.

Time is Money, *Ferdinand Danton, Jr*

An early example of an artist who used the theme was *Ferdinand Danton* (1877-1912). In 1894 he made a Trompe l'oeil painting in which he depicts an alarm clock and a stack of dollar bills, each nailed with a cord on what looks like a wooden door (oil on canvas, 43 x 53,7 cm). The two items are hanging on the same height, to emphasize the equivalence of time and money. In the middle between the clock and the dollar bills, incised in the door, is the word *is*, and below this incision is a painted ticket nailed on the wood which reads "Time is money". And if you look precisely, you can see that the *s* of the word *is* has two little notches, one at the top and one at the bottom, so that the s looks like a dollar sign: $.

Time/Bank, *Julieta Aranda and Anton Vidokle*

A modern version of Robert Owen's Labour Exchange was presented at the *Documenta 13* in Kassel (2012). Artists *Julieta Aranda* (1975, Mexico city) and *Anton Vidokle* (1965, Moscow) had established a *Time/Bank* in a pavilion. It showed an alternative currency with working hours as foundation of value. There were banknotes in many denominations, for instance half an hour, an hour, six hours or ten hours. The banknotes had been designed in different languages by various artists. The project Time/Bank started in 2010 and has got many departments all over the world meanwhile. The intention of the artists goes beyond merely showing an artwork, for they set up an online platform where people can exchange services and products based on working hours without the use of money. In their website you can find a survey of all the available skills.[240]

The artists of the Time/Bank actually return to the classical labour theory of values, as formulated by economists like Adam Smith, David Ricardo, and Karl Marx. Meanwhile similar time banks have been founded all over the world, which use a comparable exchange system of time units. The question raised by this is whether it can be argued that this kind of exchange system operates essentially different from or is principally deviating from the regular monetary exchange. In my view the answer is: no not in essence. It's just that the scale of these alternative monetary systems is smaller. But even a time bank like that is eventually based on faith, on the faith that someone else is prepared to do the job you want him to do in exchange for your time voucher. What counts in favor of a time bank, is that the price-fixing of the supplied services and products will be nearer to the 'fair price', as postulated by *Aristotle* and Christian thinkers like *Thomas of Aquino* and *Albertus Magnus*, because the participants can't cheat with inexplicable profit margins not related to working hours.

Time/Bank at e-flux is modeled on existing time banks. *Every Time/Bank transaction will allow individuals to request, offer, and pay for services in "Hour Notes". When a task is performed, the credit hours earned may be saved and used at a later date, given to another person, or contributed towards developing larger communal projects. For example, if you happen to be in Beijing or Hamburg and need someone to help you shop for materials or translate a press release, you would be able to draw on resources from Time/Bank without exchanging any money.*[241]

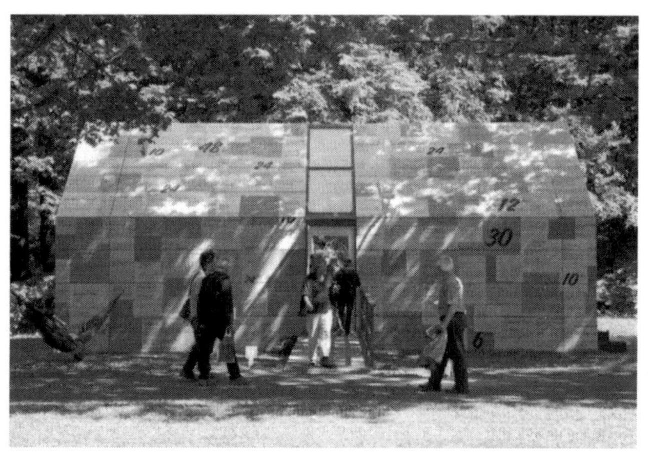

The Time/Bank pavilion at Documenta 13, Kassel 2012

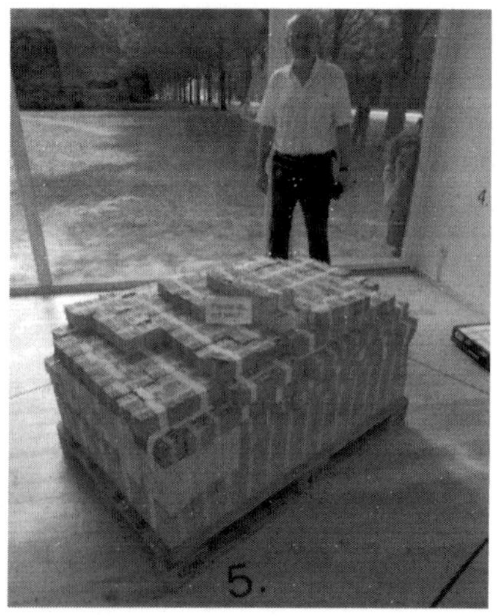

The author gazing at a stack of Time Banknotes in the Time/Bank pavilion.

Money Watching, *Cesare Pietroiusti*

In chapter one we met Italian artist *Cesare Pietroiusti* in his performance *Eating Money*. In the same year, 2007, he opened a storefront for one day, where people were invited to look concentratedly at a banknote for a couple of minutes, and when they succeeded, they could take the banknote home. In this *Money Watching* project, a banknote was housed in a glass vitrine, and a single participant was asked to watch it, until a predetermined quantity of attention, measured in time, had been given to the banknote. If adequate attention was given, the participant received the banknote. Pietroiusti displayed more than one banknote (in separate vitrines), meaning the participant had to make a choice based on the value of the banknote.

Money Watching first occurred in Birmingham, England, one of a series of performances titled "Paradoxical Economies", made for the 2007 Fierce festival. The storefront was open from 10am to 6pm for one day. Participants received a £10 note if they watched it for 15 minutes or a £20 note if they watched it for 25 minutes. The banknote was flipped over halfway through the watching. Since then *Money Watching* has occurred in other cities, like Johannesburg, Paris and Costenza (Italy).

The artist conceived the work as a way to demonstrate the arbitrary nature of the art market, and valuation more generally. He also wanted to dislodge currency from its fetish status. Its location in a storefront, set between other shops, also served to generate a basic reversal of roles: the participants who succeeded, received money instead of spending it. There is no record of the total funding distributed among participants, but many of them have received banknotes. Because of this, *Money Watching* has been listed in a database of "Arte Util" (Useful Art), hosted by the Queens Museum of Art (New York).

If your curiosity is aroused, you can look at YouTube videos of *Money Watching*.[242]

Attention: the new currency, *Christa Sommerer & Laurent Mignonneau*

Attention is a key factor contributing to the determination of the monetary value of an artwork. According to the Austrian professor *Georg Franck*, attention is the new currency in our media-based society.[243] He said that gaining attention is now even more important than earning money. Profit can be increased with the help of marketing and other attention-accumulation strategies. In Franck's opinion the cultural industry is a capital market of attention. Look at the art rankings for instance, which show the monetary value of an artist and his or her artworks. Art has become a commodity and the artist a brand name.

The artists *Christa Sommerer & Laurent Mignonneau* (1964 Austria, 1967 France) dealt with creating value by transforming user attention into monetary value. They aimed *to raise awareness of the complex topic of value creation and its link to the attention economy by physically involving the visitors in art experiments.*[244] *To do this, we transformed existing paintings that we bought at auction houses. We equipped them with sensor technology that can measure the exact time viewers spend in front of them. A small thermal printer is also attached to the frame of each painting.*[245] The artists knew the exact initial value of each system: amount paid for the painting and interface materials + value of their working time (60 Euros an hour). At the start of the exhibition, this total initial value was printed out on the paper of the thermal printer. The first painting they exhibited in 2010 in this way was called *"The Value of Art/Unruhige See"*. The initial value was € 2078.70. After several exhibitions in which a large number of visitors looked at it, in 2015 its value had increased to € 24,000.

How did they measure this? Well, they had *set the value of user attention at 1 Euro for each ten seconds. This was based on observations that the average attention span of visitors towards art works in museums lays somewhere between 4-10 seconds. The conversion of 10 seconds into 1 Euro shows visitors their immediate impact onto the work, as the painting keeps printing the new value as soon as he or she stand in front of it. Our sensor system constantly updates the value of the painting.*[246] While they watched, visitors could see how the value of the artwork increased. The longer they looked at it, the more valuable it became.

Sommerer and Mignonneau presented this artwork as an example of *Interactive Art*. It's a kind of art that became popular in the 1990s and combines *concepts of participatory art, feedback mechanisms, cybernetic principles, sensor technologies and computing processes.*[247] *Interactive Art* takes *Participatory Art* a step further, because it *interprets and transforms various sensory inputs from the audience. That can, for example, be their gestures, touch, voice input, or various other multi-modal interactions.* So the audience has a big part in the completion of the artwork. An artwork like *"The Value of Art/Unruhige See"* in fact even doesn't exist without the active participation of the viewer. According to Sommerer and Mignonneau, this active involvement of the audience *also poses a question as to the value of art itself. When the artists voluntarily retreat from their powerful position of determining the preferred interpretation of their work, they also need to consider how the value of these artworks will be determined.*[248]

But, although a lot of public attention often transforms in extra monetary value, personally I have my doubts if this also corresponds with a great quality of the exhibited artworks and artists.

8

Empire of the imagination

The fiduciary world of money and art

Credit is a form of belief. We need it for the effective functioning of our fiduciary money economy as well as the art world. Fiduciary Money is money without intrinsic value, also called Fiat Money. The paper and virtual money we use nowadays is not convertible into gold or silver. It is backed only by faith that it is an accepted medium of exchange, unit of account and store of value. Faith also was a central theme in chapter 6 (In Art we Trust), where I wrote about the religious-like *ring of believers* without whom the art world couldn't exist, and the money artists who use(d) this theme in their work.

Twentieth century economics as well as visual aesthetics has been hallmarked by an ongoing trend toward dematerialization. Between the time of the *electrum* money of ancient Ephesus and that of today's *electronic* money, there has been an ongoing development from *substantial* value to *face* value. The substantial value of money refers to the material or physical value of the currency. The face value is an intellectual, metaphysical value. This corresponds to the development from *thing* to *inscription*. This process of abstraction was accelerated with the introduction of paper money: now the *thing* was reduced from precious metal to a piece of paper and the *inscription* became the monetary sign we had to rely upon. And in the next step from tangible to intangible money, the step from banknotes to virtual, electronic money, even the link between inscription and substance was broken. *The **matter** of electronic money does **not matter***, as Shell puts it.[249]

Now that even the link between thing and inscription in virtual money is broken, what remains to guarantee that your immaterial, almost invisible, money is yours? In other words, how can you prove that your bank account is really yours? With your signature! Whether written or by way of a computer password or some other code, for every electronic monetary transaction you still have to identify yourself. Identification is the transaction to prove that you really are who you say you are, that you really exist. This applies for almost everything in life today, so also for money and art. Money that is not verified by some authorization, or art that is not certified by the signature of the artist for instance, is considered to be fraud or fake. That's why the signature of the president of the ECB is on the Euro banknotes, the signature of the Treasury Secretary on dollar bills, and the one of the Chief Cashier on the British pound notes. That's the way to reassure us that we can have faith in this fiduciary money.

A signed urinal and broken shovels, *Marcel Duchamp, Hans Haacke*

A famous artist who used this idea to transform an ordinary commodity in a work of art was *Marcel Duchamp*. In 1917 he signed a porcelain urinal with *R. Mutt*, and titled it *Fountain*. (R. Mutt was one of the pseudonyms Duchamp used, and many years later he stated that it came from the Mott Works – J.L. Mott Iron Works, manufacturer of the urinal – but was modified to Mutt, after the daily strip cartoon "Mutt and Jeff"). Originally rejected, after some time it even became collectible in replica. With this work he demonstrated that the convention of art allows the artist's signature to give aesthetic value, and so monetary value, to the humblest object. It's almost like an alchemistic transformation: the artist as *a near-miraculous creator of value, transmuting relatively relative inexpensive materials into fabulously expensive commodities.*[250] A few years earlier, in 1915, Duchamp already performed the same kind of alchemistic trick with a snow shovel. He bought it in a hardware store, signed it, hung it from the ceiling in his New York studio and gave it the title *In Advance of the Broken Arm.* The shovel thus was transformed into art. Collectors and museums eventually called for replicas, which Duchamp was happy to supply.

In 1986 the German artist *Hans Haacke* (1936, Koln) alluded to this *miraculous transformation of store-bought base metal into art-gallery gold with his gilded shovel, its handle broken well in advance of any arm.*[251] He called it *Broken R.M.*, a title and work clearly linked to Duchamp, its handle broken well in advance, and provided with a sign: *Art & Argent a tous les etages.*

An immaterial pictorial zone, *Yves Klein*

In 1959 French artist Yves Klein (1928-1962) performed a monetary artwork called *Zone de Sensibilité Picturale Immatérielle (Zone of immaterial pictorial sensibility)*. The work involved the sale of documentation of ownership of empty space: the Immaterial Zone. It took the form of a cheque, in exchange for gold, a receipt declaring the ownership of a non-existent space. The buyer of the cheque could choose what to do with it: if he wished, the piece could be completed in an elaborate ritual in which the buyer would burn the cheque, and Klein would throw half of the gold in the Seine. The ritual would be performed in the presence of an art critic or distinguished dealer, an art museum director and at least two witnesses. Here Klein offered the ownership of something truly eternal, as opposed to a piece of physical ephemerality. Between the creation of the work in 1959 and his death on June 6, 1962, eight *Zones* were sold.

With this performance, he set the invisible, imaginary stage for artists worldwide. *Klein's receipts verify the existence of an invisible work of art, which prove that a formal sale has taken place. As Klein establishes in his 'Ritual Rules', each buyer has two possibilities; if he pays the amount of gold agreed upon in exchange for a receipt, Klein keeps all of the gold, and the buyer does not really acquire the "authentic immaterial value" of the work. The second possibility is to buy an immaterial zone for gold and then to burn the receipt. Through this act, a perfect, definitive immaterialization is achieved, as well as the absolute inclusion of the buyer in the immaterial... Klein presents capitalist trading strategies and illuminates his ideas about the indefinable, incalculabe value of art.*[252]

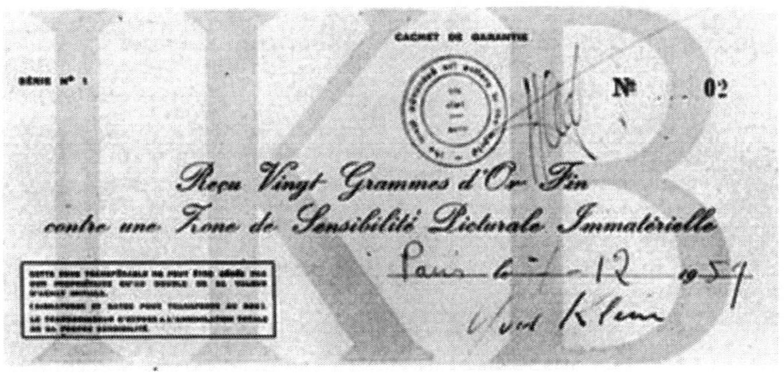

A cheque used to certify the purchase of a *Zone de Sensibilité Picturale Immatérielle*.

This copy was bought by Jacques Kugel, December 7, 1959[253]

Greed Devours, *Ralf Kopp*

On the 17th of July in 2014 the German artist *Ralf Kopp* (1973, Darmstadt) wrote the German word VERTRAUEN (Trust) with thousands of one-cent coins in public space on *Frankfurt's* shopping street *Zeil*. Each letter of the word was about one meter deep and about half a meter wide. Each letter was made of approx. 6,000 cent-coins. It was meant as a social sculpture, uncommented and unprotected. This artistic experiment was later repeated in other cities, but Frankfurt was chosen as the starting point of the action not by accident: Frankfurt is *the Bank city that is struggling and advertising for confidence of the financial markets,* Ralf Kopp said.[254] He wanted to know how people react when they see money in public space, unprotected, easy to grab. *Is "TRUST" stronger than the power of money? Does "greed" destroy "TRUST"? Or does the meaning of the word protect the installation against being destructed? Does someone add money because of the importance of the word? The viewer will inevitably make thoughts about his relationship with the words content and the material with which the word is written.*[255]

How do you think people reacted when they saw the money in this public space, easy to grab? Well, I think you can guess: the *Vertrauen* was gone within a day. Several pedestrians took money from the unprotected artwork, but some others *put down some of their own money instead of taking some. Several visitors even took their time and rearranged the piles of coins when others destroyed them by walking over the artwork.*[256]

Kopp repeated the concept of "Greed devours" in several cities with other positive words, like "culture" (greed devours: CULTURE), "art", "freedom" or "democracy" and many more words, and in different languages. The word FREEDOM for instance, was written in the same way on the 18th of September 19, 2014, in Berlin. The artist wondered what would happen to the coins in Berlin. *Will the greed destroy* ***freedom*** *and thus return the artistic material to the circulation of money?* – well, the *freedom* was completely gone after 12 hours. *Despite the numerous efforts to reorder the letters, the* ***freedom*** *hardly survived the day. The more difficult it was to recognize the word, the lesser people hesitated to "steal" the money from the pile.*[257]

Paying people to do crazy things, *Santiago Sierra*
Spanish artist *Santiago Sierra* (1966) is known for his works involving hiring laborers to complete menial tasks. *These works are meant to elucidate the nature of the laborer within Capitalist society, how the laborer sells his physical labor and thus his body.*[258] Sierra is critical of capitalism and the institutions which support it, and makes art about political issues like immigrant poverty in Capitalist countries and the isolation of economic classes. *Drawing on the art-historical tradition of using paid models, often taken from the streets, Sierra commissioned his models from the unwanted and ostracized – street workers, illegal immigrants, the unemployed and dispossessed.*[259]

In 2002 he hired a beggar in Birmingham to stand on New Street and say: *My participation in this piece could generate a profit of 72,000 dollars. I am being paid five pounds.* What did the beggar think of this discrepancy between his humble reward and the anticipated huge profit for the artist? Well, he didn't appear unduly indignant. Neither was he worried about the political or artistic implications of the statement. No, *he was presumably quite happy to accept a fiver for his efforts.*[260] Possibly the artist wanted to *expose the myth that most participatory artworks are inherently generous, by showing ways that they are potentially self-serving and often profoundly unequal in terms of who benefits from their production*, Ted Purves and Shane Aslan Selzer wrote.[261]

In previous actions Sierra had never shortage of workers willing to be paid for participation in his works. For instance: once he paid a museum watchman in PS1 (MoMA) in New York to live behind a brick wall for 365 hours (= 15 days). Did the watchman mind? No, on the contrary, the man told Sierra *that no one had ever been so interested in him and that he had never met so many people.*[262]

Then there were the four heroin-addicted prostitutes he hired in 2000 in Salamanca, Spain. Sierra paid them 12,000 pesetas each, the price of one dose of heroin. What did the artist ask them to do? They had to sit next to each other on stools, face to the wall, their backs naked. Then Sierra tattooed a horizontal 160 cm line across the worker's backs, a work he called *160 cm Line Tattooed on Four People.* Spectators of the performance looked at it with some horror, but how did the four ladies react while the artist was tattooing? Well, during the realization of the work, they were casually chatting to each other.

In 2010 Sierra did a project, called *7 forms measuring 600 x 60 x 60 cm constructed to be held horizontal to a wall.* For this *Project 22*, seven black coffin-like forms were supported upon the shoulders of paid workers throughout the exhibition period from 20 -28 November in the *Gallery of Modern Art* at Brisbane. A total of 28 workers were involved each day, and *Sierra stipulated that they must be paid the minimum wage and be genuinely in need of work. Positioned in the gallery space, side-by-side, the seven forms, and fourteen workers who hold them, created a serial, repetitive, appearance, dividing the gallery into 'those who work and those who watch'.* [263] The bearers of the coffin-like forms *recall the caryatid or atlas figures whose sculpted forms stand as pillars to support the weight of classical architecture. Carrying casket-like forms on their shoulders, they represent what Sierra calls the 'social burial' of labor.*[264]

Other examples of Sierra's work involve the tattooing of six unemployed young men in Havana, Cuba, for the sum of 30 US dollars each (1999), a work he already did before the "160 cm Line" on the four Ladies' backs. For the Venice Biennale in 2001, he paid 133 illegal street vendors, immigrants from China, Senegal and Bangladesh, to dye their hair blonde. But besides these relative innocent actions, Sierra also provoked people with rather revolting actions like *ten people paid to masturbate* (Havana, 2000) or a so called investigation in sexual variations, using different coupling of race and gender in his work *Los Penetrados* (2009).

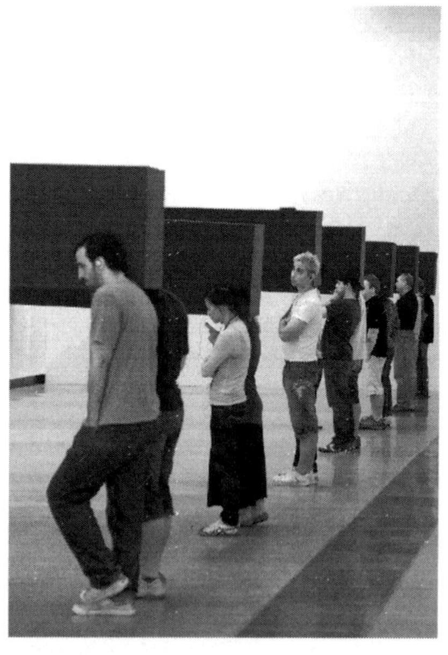

Santiago Sierra, *7 forms measuring 600 x 60 x 60 cm constructed to be held horizontal to a wall (2010)*

Take what you need, *Lee Lozano*

In 1969 American painter and visual and conceptual artist *Lee Lozano* (1930-1999) offered a jar full of money to artists who visited her in her New York studio. At the beginning the jar contained bills of $5, $10 and $20, with a total amount of about $585, coiled in two or three packets around the inside of the jar, unbound. She got the money from artist Rolf Ricke, who had sold his painting "Switch".[265] Her visitors could either contribute or extract funds at will. They were offered coffee, diet pepsi, bourbon, glass of half and half, ice water, grass, and money. The money was in an open jar and offered like candy. Lozano called her performance *Real Money Piece,* a jarring piece. This "chain piece" took place over the course of 3-4 months, from April to July 1969, and during that time the artist recorded what transpired as she offered the jar full of money to a range of visitors. The indication "chain piece" stood for the visitors part in the piece: everyone who took money out of the jar, had to decide what to do with it: Keep it? Return it? Give it away? How did they react? Their reactions became a document of the visiting artists' different opinions about money and its distribution.

I give you some examples of how the artists reacted:[266]
Apr 15: Ron Kleeman takes out a $20. He wishes to put it back into the jar, but I talk him into keeping it.
Apr 17: Keith Sonnier refused, later screws lid very tightly back on.
Apr 27: Kaltenbach takes all the money out of the jar when I offer it, examines all the money & puts it all back in jar. Says he doesn't need the money now.
Apr 28: David Parson refused, laughing.

May 1: Warren C. Ingersoll refused. He got very upset about my "attitude towards money".

May 4: Keith Sonnier refused, but said he would take money if he needed it which he might in the future.

May 7: Dick Anderson barely glances at the money when I stick it under his nose and says: "Oh no thanks, I intend to earn it on my own."

...

May 10: Dan Graham puts $50 into the jar (to repay loan).

May 12: Abe Lubelski refrains, says he's expecting a big check soon, income tax return (I think).

May 13: Paul Bianchini declines until he "ask his wife", then asks me why I have money in a brown jar. Simone Stern (who has a gallery in New Orleans) says she doesn't care to have any now, "Too salty".

...

May 20: David Lee takes $1. (Note: Start new method of first removing all bills from jar, spread them out & offer a free choice of various denominations: "deck of cards" method.

May 22: John Torreano doesn't want any money (says he doesn't need it now) but he takes the jar! Hooray!

May 23: Paula Davies and Marilyn Learner drop in unexpectedly. Neither take any lace but Paula later says she was "controlling herself".

May 25: Alan Saret takes all the money for a minute but I must have had an expression of terror on my face because he puts it all back.

…

May 28: Claire Copley doesn't take any, she seems insulted & offended that I offer it to her (in such a 'vulgar' way?)

…

June 6: Alan Saret visits again & makes a Piece of the money which is now in two piles on the floor, each shaped similarly to a "footstep" by folding & molding to his hand. It looks good like that & I'm gonna leave it on the floor for a while.

…

July 9: Arthur Berman who is flat broke will only take 20 cents for his subway fare home.

What did Lee Lozano do with her record of all the visitors' reactions? She wrote it down with ink and graphite on notebook papers and exhibited them.

Forty years later, in 2009, the *Real Money Piece* of Lee Lozano was reinterpreted as a kind of tribute in a performance by *Elana Mann* (1980, Boston) in Los Angeles, called *Real Money Peace 1969/2009*. She offered her visitors the same variety of things (coffee, diet pepsi, bourbon, half and half, ice water – but "grass" from Lozano's original instructions was omitted), and again a jar filled with money, from the sale of Mann's artwork. A number of people came through and interacted with the artist. Like in the performance of Lozano, each interaction was documented through written text, this time on a large sheet of durable paper. But while Lozano's project took place over the course of 3-4 months, Mann's lasted only 3-4 hours. *Money flowed out of and back into the jar, and seemed to become something other than money, released as it was from its customarily cold, cut-and-dry exchange policies,* Dan Graham wrote.[267]

Outro

When I give a power point lecture on **Money Art & Artificial Money**, many listeners and viewers are astonished. They didn't have any idea of the existence of such artists. Artists in the past who were inspired by money, and contemporary artists who use it as an idea or material to create works of money art, and even specialize in it. Of course, many people have heard of famous artists like *Andy Warhol* with his *Dollar Signs* or *Quentin Massijs* with his iconic *Money Changer and his Wife*, and when I show them the *Danaë* painting of *Gustav Klimt*, it rings a bell, but who the hell is *Cayman* or *Jonone100*? What are they up to? The one is putting shredded money in crystal balls and the other is in the habit of burning money. Why? And then there is the guy that's eating money and another who was hiding gold bars at the beach. Eating money? Ugh! And then waiting for the swallowed notes to be evacuated and returned to the successful bidder... phew! Is that art?

All those artists are in the business of money art, but many contemporary artists don't seem to paint anymore – they are performing conceptual art. Sometimes it looks like they are playing with money. Some of them are folding

Moneygami artworks, others are cutting and gluing money collages or they make dogs, weapons and dresses with it.

Writing this book was a voyage of discovery. A voyage with often unexpected views on money art and artists who I hadn't heard of before, but are famous in their own field. I hope that with this book I've opened and widened a spy hole for readers on the world of money art.

Further reading

Beuys, Joseph, et al., *What is Money? – A discussion*, United Kingdom, 2010

Büchner, Hermann and Sauerländer, Tina (Eds.), *SAMMLUNG HAUPT, Dreißig Silberlinge – Kunst und Geld*, Berlin, 2013

Capeloa Gil, Isabel and Gonçalves da Silva, Helena (Eds.), *The Cultural Life of Money*, Berlin/Boston, 2015

Crostwaite, Paul; Knight, Peter and Marsh, Nicky (Eds.), *Show me The Money – The Image of Finance, 1700 to the present*, Manchester/New York, 2014

Dossi, Piroschka, ***Hype!*** *– Kunst und Geld*, München, 2007

Haiven, Max, *Cultures of Financialization – Fictitious Capital in Popular Culture and Everyday Life*, New York, 2014

Harris, Jonathan, *Money Burner's Manual – A Guide to Ritual Sacrifice*, Hertfordshire, 2017

Harten, Jürgen, a.o., *Museum des Geldes – Über die seltsame Natur des Geldes in Kunst, Wissenschaft und Leben*, Düsseldorf, 1978

Hattinger, Gottfried (Hg.), *Sozialmaschine Geld – Kunst. Positionen*, Frankfurt am Main, 2000

Huber, Thomas, *Der Duft des Geldes – Die Bank, Eine Wertvorstellung*, Darmstadt, 1992

Italiaander, Rolf; Gundermann, Hans and Büchner, Joachim, *Geld in der Kunst – Geld und Geldeswert in Skulptur, Graphik und Malerei*, Hannover, 1951

Pircher, Wolfgang (Hg.), *Sozialmaschine Geld – Kultur. Geschichte*, Frankfurt am Main, 2000

Purves, Ted and Selzer, Shane Aslan (Eds.), *What we want is free – Critical Exchanges in Recent Art*, New York, 2014

Raap, Jürgen a.o., *DAS SCHICKSAL DES GELDES, Kunst und Geld – Eine Bilanz zum Jahrtausendwechsel*, in: KUNSTFORUM International, Band 149, Köln, März 2000

Shell, Marc, *Art & Money*, Chicago, 1995

Siegel, Katy and Mattick, Paul, *Art Works – Money*, New York, 2004

Velthuis, Olav, *Imaginary Economics*, Rotterdam, 2005

Weschler, Lawrence, *BOGGS – A Comedy of Values*, Chicago and London, 2000

Widemann, Reinold, *Money is a Mind Thing – On Symbols of Value*, Soesterberg, 2016

Yamey, Basil S., *Art & Accounting*, New Haven & London, 1989

Endnotes

1 http://geldkunst.blogspot.nl/
2 http://berlin-china-echo.blogspot.nl/2010/04/money-money.html
3 http://geldkunst.blogspot.nl/
4 https://en.wikipedia.org/wiki/Hell_money
5 http://www.dox.cz/en/exhibitions/the-soul-of-money
6 http://www.skd.museum/en/special-exhibitions/archive/supermarket-of-the-dead/index.html
7 http://jmrhiggs.blogspot.nl/2013/11/ten-reasons-for-burning-money.html
8 https://www.quora.com/Why-does-The-Joker-burn-the-money-in-The-Dark-Knight
9 https://en.wikipedia.org/wiki/Discordianism
10 Ibid.
11 The Fortean Society started in the U.S. in 1931 in order to promote the ideas of American writer Charles Fort.
http://jonone100.blogspot.nl/2013/10/money-burning-at-horse-hospital.html
12 https://medium.com/@jonone100/money-burning-ritual-at-f23-fc7e256e920a
13 https://medium.com/@jonone100/money-burning-ritual-at-f23-fc7e256e920a
14 John Higgs, *The KLF: Chaos, Magic and the Band who Burned a Million Pounds*, London 2013, Orion Publishing Group.
15 See for instance: https://en.wikipedia.org/wiki/The_KLF
16 www.lysator.liu.se/~johol/KLF/Money.htm
17 Ibid.
18 www.lysator.liu.se/~johol/KLF/Money.htm
19 www.lysator.liu.se/~johol/KLF/Money.htm

20 http://ftp.xmission.com/pub/users/l/lazlo/music/klf/news-reviews/kfoundation-19940925-observer-burn.txt
21 www.lysator.liu.se/~johol/KLF/Money.htm
22 http://www.dreadscott.net/works/money-to-burn/
23 http://franklinfurnace.org/artists/franklin_furnace_fund/
24 http://www.dreadscott.net/works/money-to-burn/
25 https://www.hkw.de/en/programm/projekte/veranstaltung/p_98741.php
26 http://granaton.com/hello-bitcoin/
27 http://geraldine.juarez.se/bouquet.html
28 http://fffff.at/some-people-just-want-to-see-the-market-crash
29 http://amarist.com/artwork/
30 http://freshome.com/2014/07/18/provoking-money-burning-table-too-much-by-alejandro-monge/
31 Ibid.
32 Ibid.
33 http://www.italianarea.it/opera.php?w=PIEC_55.jpg&artista=PIEC&let=
34 http://www.ic.mmoma.ru/en/artists/cesarepietroiusti
35 Marc Shell, Art & Money, p. 15, 1995.
36 http://www.franzgratwohl.ch/doku/VideoEn.pdf
37 http://www.nbk.org/en/video-forum/Franz_Gratwohl_Stefan_Halter.html
38 http://www.franzgratwohl.ch/doku/VideoEn.pdf
39 www.louvre.fr/en/oeuvre-notices/moneylender-and-his-wife
40 The Guardian, 4/10/2013
41 https://thewadsworth.org/wp-content/uploads/2011/06/Matrix-86.pdf
42 Robert Hughes, "On Art and Money", The New York Review of Books, December 6, 1984, p. 20.
43 "Francesca Gavin profiles Sylvie Fleury, art's high queen of fashion and fetish" on http://www.contemporary-magazines.com/profile63.htm
44 www.ropac.net/
45 'Participation', edited by Claire Bishop. https://mitpress.mit.edu/books/participation
46 https://en.wikipedia.org/wiki/Danaë and www.greekmythology.com/Myths/Mortals/Danae/danae.html
47 http://www.conceptualism-moscow.org/page?id=1740&lang=eng
48 http://totallyhistory.com/danae-gustav-klimt/
49 http://www.wga.hu/html_m/c/correggi/mytholog/danae.html

50 http://www.uffizi.org/artworks/annunciation-by-simone-martini-and-lippo-memmi/

51 http://www.modernedition.com/art-articles/new-contemporary-sculpture/alicja-kwade.html

52 For explanation of this concept, see for instance: Reinold Widemann, *Money is a Mind Thing – On Symbols of Value,* chapter 8, Aspekt Publishers 2016.

53 http://historicalamericanart.blogspot.nl/2011/11/victor-dubreuil-his-life-details-and.html

54 http://blogs.artinfo.com/lacmonfire/2011/12/16/crystal-bridges-buys-cross-of-gold/

55 http://leroybrothers.com/portfolio_page/art-for-money-money-for-art/

56 https://creators.vice.com/en_us/article/panning-for-gold-money-art

57 Andy Warhol, *The Philosophy of Andy Warhol (From A to B and Back Again)*, Orlando 1975.

58 http://www.sothebys.com/en/auctions/ecatalogue/2015/contemporary-art-evening-auction-l15022/lot.25.html

59 http://www.businessinsider.com/andy-warhols-painting-of-a-dollar-bill-sold-for-328-million-2015-7?international=true&r=US&IR=T

60 Megan Cohen, *Historical Echoes: Andy Warhol and the Art of Money* in 'Liberty Street Economics', July 12, 2013. http://libertystreeteconomics.newyorkfed.org/2013/07/historical-echoes-andy-warhol-and-the-art-of-money-.html

61 Arthur C. Danto, *Andy Warhol and the Love of $$$$$*, in: Exhibition Catalogue, Beverly Hills, Gagosian Gallery, *Andy Warhol: Dollar Signs*, 1997, p. 5).

62 https://theartsjournal.org/index.php/site/article/viewFile/173/206

63 Grayson Earle, *A Moment Outside: A Study of Alexander Brener's Daring Escape from the Dictates of the Western Art Market* in: Journal of Arts and Humanities (JAH), Volume -3, No.-1, January, 2014.

64 Ibid., p. 28.

65 http://www.luxuo.com/culture/art/piece-of-art-ever-made.html

66 https://www.treehugger.com/corporate-responsibility/dollar-bills-make-good-art.html

67 http://observer.com/2011/09/the-hugo-boss-prize-2010-hans-peter-feldman-has-people-with-their-eyes-on-the-prize/

68 Ibid.

69 Ibid.

70 http://www.huffingtonpost.com/adrian-margaret-brune/the-new-moneyed-art_b_918483.html

71 http://mymodernmet.com/the-dollar-bill-surgeon-12/

72 http://hifructose.com/2012/10/10/scott-campbells-skulls-made-out-of-us-currency/

73 http://www.artrepublic.com/biographies/246-justine-smith.html

74 http://www.justinesmith.net/about/

75 Ibid.

76 http://fromyourdesks.com/2013/01/07/justine-smith/

77 http://www.justinesmith.net/sculpture/weapons/

78 http://www.justinesmith.net/sculpture/coins/

79 http://www.justinesmith.net/collage/money_maps/

80 Mark Wagner, *Look sharp...the philosophy and practice of collage*, MarkWagnerInc. 2016.

81 http://markwagnerinc.com/information/

82 Ibid.

83 https://www.artsy.net/artwork/mark-wagner-very-expensive-push-broom

84 http://www.huffingtonpost.com/adrian-margaret-brune/the-new-moneyed-art_b_918483.html

85 https://vimeo.com/79148964

86 http://markwagnerinc.com/blog/

87 https://www.yahoo.com/news/photos/alternating-currency-the-currency-collages-of-c-k-wilde-slideshow/

88 https://www.artsy.net/artist/c-dot-k-wilde

89 Ibid.

90 http://origamido.com/who-we-are/index.html

91 http://inhabitat.com/sipho-mabonas-swarming-origami-locusts-are-made-of-money/mabona-origami1/

92 https://www.yatzer.com/The-Plague-Installation-by-Sipho-Mabona-Money-Origami

93 Ibid.

94 Ibid.

95 https://www.flickr.com/photos/sipmab/

96 https://origami.wonderhowto.com/news/make-abe-lincoln-look-like-b-boy-5-dollar-bill-origami-0124246/

97 http://www.nationmultimedia.com/news/sunday/aec/30265660

98 Ibid.

99 Ibid.

100 http://installationmag.com/dan-tague-plates-slides/

101 Ibid.

102 https://www.treehugger.com/corporate-responsibility/dollar-bills-make-good-art.html

103 Ibid.

104 http://installationmag.com/dan-tague-plates-slides/

105 https://www.judgerealty.com/blog/tag/jason-hughes/

106 http://www.citypaper.com/arts/visualart/bcpnews-cash-rules-jason-hughes-terms-conditions-makes-money-into-art-20150407-story.html

107 https://www.judgerealty.com/blog/tag/jason-hughes/

108 https://hyperallergic.com/134218/shredding-currency-in-the-name-of-art/

109 http://www.thebubble.com/arteba-the-man-who-shredded-a-million-dollars/

110 Friedrich Nietzsche, *On the Genealogy of Morals*, 1887

111 http://www.thebubble.com/arteba-the-man-who-shredded-a-million-dollars/

112 https://www.theatlantic.com/international/archive/2014/06/why-i-shredded-1-million-dollars-argentina-economy/372882/

113 Ibid.

114 Ibid.

115 Ibid.

116 Benjamin J. Cohen, *The Geography of Money*, 1998

117 Reinold Widemann, *Money is a Mind Thing – On Symbols of Value*, 2016, p. 103, Soesterberg Nederland, Aspekt Publishers.

118 Isabel Capeloa Gil, Helena Gonçalves da Silva (Eds.), *The Cultural Life of Money,* 2015, Berlin/Boston, De Gruyter.

119 http://bitterqueen.typepad.com/friends_of_ours/2016/10/culture-vultures-mafia-steals-art-for-use-as-currency.html

120 http://observer.com/2012/03/its-a-bird-its-a-plane-its-another-art-fair/

121 http://www.artmarketmonitor.com/2012/03/07/art-as-a-currency/

122 https://www.askart.com/art/styles/20/y/trompe%20l'oeil

123 http://www.nytimes.com/1988/11/25/business/money-is-the-subject-art-the-object.html?pagewanted=all

124 Ibid.

125 https://www.nga.gov/feature/artnation/harnett/money_3.shtm

126 http://www.coinworld.com/news/paper-money/2015/07/temptation--illusion-and-deception--dubreuil-s-paper-money-art.all.html#

127 Ibid.

128 http://www.coinbooks.org/esylum_v18n29a25.html
129 https://fineart.ha.com/itm/fine-art-painting/the-hon-paul-h-buchanan-jr-collection-victor-dubreuil-american-circa-1880-1900-american-paper-curr/a/5024-77034.s?ic4=ListView-Thumbnail-071515
130 Marc Shell, *Art & Money*, Chicago and London 1995, The University of Chicago Press.
131 Ibid.
132 http://historicalamericanart.blogspot.nl/2011/11/victor-dubreuil-his-life-details-and.html
133 http://www.coinworld.com/news/paper-money/2015/07/temptation--illusion-and-deception--dubreuil-s-paper-money-art.all.html#
134 Ibid.
135 Ibid.
136 https://www.nga.gov/feature/artnation/harnett/haberle.htm
137 Ibid.
138 https://en.wikipedia.org/wiki/John_Haberle
139 https://www.nga.gov/feature/artnation/harnett/haberle.htm
140 Alfred Frankenstein, *After the Hunt: William Michael Harnett and Other Still Life Painters, 1870-1900*, 2nd ed., Berkeley and Los Angeles, 1968.
141 http://www.brockandco.com/meurer_slwmpl_h.html
142 https://en.wikipedia.org/wiki/William_Harnett
143 https://www.nga.gov/feature/artnation/harnett/money_1.shtm
144 Ibid.
145 http://www.brockandco.com/meurer_slwmpl_h.html
146 http://www.internetantiquegazette.com/paintings/3126_charles_alfred_meurer_american_artist_tromp_loeil_artist/
147 A. Frankenstein, *After the Hunt: William Michael Harnett and Other Still Life Painters, 1870-1900*, 2nd ed., Berkeley and Los Angeles, 1968, p. 154-155.
148 http://www.brockandco.com/meurer_slwmpl_h.html
149 https://www.wsj.com/articles/review-of-otis-kaye-money-mystery-and-mastery-at-the-new-britain-museum-of-american-art-1426112375
150 Ibid.
151 Ibid.
152 Ibid.
153 Ibid.
154 Ibid.
155 http://blog.ha.com/2015/09/from-pocket-change-to-work-of-art-trompe-loeil-and-paper-money/

156 Ibid.

157 Lawrence Weschler, *Boggs: A Comedy of Values*, Chicago and London 2000, The University of Chicago Press.

158 Ibid.

159 Ibid.

160 https://www.economist.com/news/obituary/21716015-artist-and-trickster-was-62-obituary-jsgboggs-was-found-dead-january-23rd

161 John Stuart Mill, *Principals of Political Economy, with Some of their Applications to Social Philosophy*, 1848.

162 http://www.susanstockwell.co.uk/about.php

163 http://www.designboom.com/art/susan-stockwell-folds-a-fleet-of-ships-from-global-currency-11-29-2013/

164 Ibid.

165 Ibid.

166 Ibid.

167 http://www.susanstockwell.co.uk/medium.php?image_id=2010-07-17-7

168 Ibid.

169 *Maria Fisahn: Geld(aus)Tausch*, in: Kunstforum Bd. 149, Januar-März 2000

170 http://financeandsociety.ed.ac.uk/article/view/1370/1899

171 http://www.maximogonzalez.info/piezas_hechas_con_dinero/magma.php?lang=en

172 http://www.maximogonzalez.info/piezas_hechas_con_dinero/magma.php

173 Ibid.

174 http://financeandsociety.ed.ac.uk/article/view/1370/1899

175 http://www.leemingwei.com/projects.php#

176 http://www.aaa-a.org/programs/presentation-by-lee-mingwei/

177 Ibid.

178 Sammlung Haupt, Dreißig Silberlinge – Kunst und Geld; herausgegeben von Hermann Büchner und Tina Sauerländer, Edition Braus Berlin, 2013.

179 http://www.leemingwei.com/projects.php#

180 https://www.therealreal.com/products/women/objects-barton-benes

181 http://www.artnet.com/artists/barton-lidice-benes/haute-cuisine-Xu2Hwi4QQVDzzIxBndwuZQ2

182 https://www.ebth.com/items/5954679-barton-lidice-benes-mixed-media-money-lighthouse

183 https://www.wikiart.org/en/barton-lidice-benes/afghanistan-2001

184 https://en.wikipedia.org/wiki/William_Powhida

185 https://maxhaiven.com/2015/07/04/three-aesthetic-strategies/

186 http://blogs.reuters.com/felix-salmon/2010/12/28/a-guide-to-the-market-oligopoly-system/

187 Ibid.

188 Ibid.

189 Matt Taibbi, *Griftopia: Bubble Machines, Vampire Squids, and the Long Con That Is Breaking America* (2010). Wikipedia comments: The book argues that the financial crisis of 2008 was not an accident of the free market, but the result of a complex and ongoing politico-financial process taking place in the United States whereby wealth and power is transferred to a super-rich "grafter class" that holds grip on the political process. (...) The book contests the notion that the greed of the American consumer was a primary cause of the problem.

190 Paul Crosthwaite a/o, *Show Me The Money – The Image Of Finance, 1700 to the present* (2014).

191 Ibid.

192 http://irenebrination.typepad.com/irenebrination_notes_on_a/2012/11 /dadara-exchanghibition-bank.html

193 http://irenebrination.typepad.com/irenebrination_notes_on_a/2012/11 /dadara-exchanghibition-bank.html

194 https://en.wikipedia.org/wiki/Dadara

195 The Burning Man Festival is a yearly festival in Nevada's Black Rock Desert to create Black Rock City, a temporary metropolis dedicated to community, art, self-expression, and self-reliance.

196 http://www.dadara.nl/sculptures-and-installations/transformoney-tree

197 http://www.royalgazette.com/arts-and-entertainment/article/20160711/turning-money-into-art

198 Ibid.

199 Ibid.

200 http://www.dispatch.com/content/stories/life_and_entertainment /2014 /10/12/01-value-judgments.html

201 Ibid.

202 See also: Reinold Widemann, *Money is a Mind Thing – On Symbols of Value*, 2016, Aspekt Publishers.

203 http://www.dispatch.com/content/stories/life_and_entertainment/2014/10/12/01-value-judgments.html

204 http://www.dailyserving.com/2014/10/in-___we-trust-art-and-money-at-the-columbus-museum-of-art/

205 The phrase 'The Medium is the Message' was introduced in McLuhan's book *Understanding Media: The Extensions of Man*, published in 1964.
206 Marc Shell, *Art & Money*, 1995, Chicago and London, p. 126.
207 http://www.huffingtonpost.com/anna-deavere-smith/in-art-we-trust_b_3521724.html
208 Marc Shell, *Art & Money*, 1995, Chicago and London, p. 116.
209 http://caleblarsen.com/10000-sculpture-in-progress/
210 Ibid.
211 Ibid.
212 Ibid.
213 Bernard of Clairvaux, *Letter to Art and Theology*. Cited from Katy Siegel and Paul Mattick, *Art Works – Money*, London 2004, Thames & Hudson.
214 Ibid.
215 https://www.ubs.com/microsites/art_collection/home/the-collection/a-z/informations/gursky-andreas/99_cent.html
216 https://www.thefreelibrary.com/%22Shopping%22%3A+Schirn+ Kunst halle.+(Frankfurt).-a0101779225
217 http://articles.latimes.com/2013/aug/23/news/la-art-review-liquid-assets-by-ari-gersht-20130823
218 Ibid.
219 http://www.yesmagazine.org/new-economy/peoples-bailout-just-the-beginning-whats-next-strike-debt-rolling-jubilee
220 If you want to know more about ABS (Asset Backed Securities), see my book *Bankzaken – Economie van Commercial Banking (Banking Business – Economics of Commercial Banking)*, only available in Dutch, Convoy Publishers, Dordrecht.
221 https://www.artprize.org/thomas-gokey/2011/total-amount-of-money-rendered-in-exchange-for-a-masters-of-fine-arts-degree-to-the-school-of-the-ar
222 http://superflex.net/tools/bankrupt_banks/image
223 http://www.thedailybeast.com/blame-the-graphic-designers
224 http://www.art-agenda.com/reviews/superflex-bankrupt-banks/
225 https://chantalpowell.wordpress.com/2009/02/14/how-to-build-cathedrals-cildo-meireles-1987/
226 Ibid.
227 https://www.theguardian.com/artanddesign/2008/oct/11/cildo-meireles
228 http://tyrusclutter.blogspot.nl/2010/11/cildo-meireles-expositor-of-brazils.html

229 http://www.tate.org.uk/art/artworks/meireles-insertions-into-ideological-circuits-2-banknote-project-t12526
230 Ibid.
231 Ibid.
232 https://www.moma.org/collection/works/81983
233 Ibid.
234 Ibid.
235 https://zoowithoutanimals.com/tag/money-tree/
236 Ibid.
237 http://www.macba.cat/en/zero-dollar-3806
238 http://e-flux.com/timebank/about
239 Adam Smith, *The Wealth of Nations*, originally 1776, New York 2003: Bantam Classic.
240 http://e-flux.com/timebank/about
241 Ibid.
242 https://www.youtube.com/watch?v=LoUqlY7ULNg
243 Georg Franck, *Ökonomie der Aufmerksamkeit, ein Entwurf*, München 1998, Edition Akzente, Hanser Verlag.
244 See their informative article **"The Value of Art" – Transforming User Attention into Monetary Value in a Series of Interactive Artworks"** on: http://isea2015.org/proceeding/submissions/ISEA2015_submission_111.pdf
245 Ibid.
246 Ibid.
247 Ibid.
248 Ibid.
249 Marc Shell, *Art & Money*, 1995, Chicago and London, p 108
250 Katy Siegel and Paul Mattick, *Art Works, Money*, New York 2004, Thames & Hudson.
251 Ibid.
252 https://en.wikipedia.org/wiki/Zone_de_Sensibilit%C3%A9_Picturale_Immat%C3%A9rielle, referring to Hatje Kantz, *Yves Klein, Berggruen Hollein & Pfeiffer*, 2004, p. 221.
253 Ibid.
254 https://vimeo.com/102079878
255 Ibid.
256 http://www.art-scene.tv/en/news/details/datum/2014/09/22/kunst-und-geld-weg.html
257 Ibid.

258 https://en.wikipedia.org/wiki/Santiago_Sierra

259 http://kaldorartprojects.org.au/projects/project-22-santiago-sierra

260 http://www.contemporary-magazines.com/reviews38_2.htm

261 Ted Purves and Shane Aslan Selzer, *What we want is free – Critical Exchanges in Recent Art*, New York, 2014.

262 https://en.wikipedia.org/wiki/Santiago_Sierra

263 http://kaldorartprojects.org.au/projects/project-22-santiago-sierra

264 Ibid.

265 http://moneyandart.tumblr.com/post/50741935031/lee-lozano-real-money-piece-1969

266 Quoted from: http://ex-fandes60s.blogspot.nl/2010/03/lee-lozanos-real-money-piece.html

267 https://anotherrighteoustransfer.wordpress.com/2009/12/07/1969-organized-by-vincent-ramos-for-the-friends-of-distinction-dan-graham-december-5-2009/